MEATS, FISH and FOWL
with Schmecks Appeal

EDNA STAEBLER

To John &
Happy Cooking

Edna Staebler

McGraw-Hill Ryerson
Montreal   Toronto

McClelland & Stewart
Toronto

First published in 1990 by

McGraw-Hill Ryerson Limited
330 Progress Avenue
Toronto, Canada
M1P 2Z5

McClelland & Stewart Limited
481 University Avenue
Suite 900
Toronto, Canada
M5G 2E9
ISBN 0-7710-8280-0

1 2 3 4 5 6 7 8 9 0 W 9 8 7 6 5 4 3 2 1 0

Canadian Cataloguing in Publication Data
Staebler, Edna, – date
  Meats, fish and fowl with schmecks appeal

(Schmecks appeal cookbook series)
ISBN 0-7710-8280-0

1. Cookery (Meat).   2. Cookery (Fish).
3. Cookery (Poultry).   4. Cookery, Mennonite.
5. Cookery – Ontario – Waterloo (Region municipality).
I. Title.   II. Series: Staebler, Edna,   – date
Schmecks appeal cookbook series.

TX749.S84 1990 641.6'6 C90-095475-2

Printed and bound in Canada

∞ This book was manufactured using acid-free paper.

CONTENTS

MEATS

*In my favourite butcher's shop in Kitchener, I heard a
customer complain: "One day I have beef, the next day
pork, on Friday fish, on Sunday chicken, and that's it.
What else is there? Lamb in the spring and turkey for
Christmas."*

*"Ach, lady, we got lots more than that yet," the butcher
told her. "There's pigs' tails and ribs, liverwurst,
kalbsbrust, schwadamagha sausage, braunschweiger. I
could easily name you seventy-five different kinds we got
right here in this shop. You got only to take home and cook
it."*

*There are no directions for cooking meat in the
handwritten cookbooks of either Mother or my friend
Bevvy Martin. Any woman in Waterloo County, who lives
in a home where meat is eaten three times a day, just
naturally knows how to prepare it.*

*Mother never used anything but the best cuts her butcher
could send her, and cooked in her own unorthodox way;
they had a more wonderful flavour than I have ever
encountered elsewhere. Steaks, chops, veal cutlets, calves'
liver, even hamburgers and bacon, she fried in butter. She
never braised or broiled anything. She never made stews
or casseroles. She didn't like mixtures. She didn't like
leftover meat; she always gave it away to her cleaning
lady. Beef dripping, chicken fat, and gravy she threw into
the garbage. Mother was a city woman. She had no thrifty
Mennonite ancestors.*

*But I have, one of my father's great-grandfathers was a
pioneering Mennonite, and now, almost two hundred years
later, when I visit my Mennonite friends the Martins, they
often say: "Edna, you got a lot of old Mennonite in you
yet"—even though my great-grandfather married an Irish
woman and the family hasn't been Mennonite since.*

1

BEEF

ROAST BEEF

"All you have to do is sprinkle the roast with salt and pepper, then put it in the oven at 350°F until the meat thermometer stuck into the centre reaches 160°F. You don't have to baste it." That's what I told Margot, the pretty, eager young woman who was our maid until we finally had to tell her we thought she'd be happier working in an office, as she had in Hamburg, Germany, before she came to us after the Second World War.

Margot took me at my word: she put the five-pound sirloin roast on the top rack of the oven without putting it into a roasting pan. Fortunately, I caught it before it started to cook.

If I hadn't tried to simplify my directions for Margot, I might have put the roast in the oven at 450°F for half an hour, then reduced the heat to 300°F until the thermometer reached 160°F for medium (140°F for rare, 170°F for well done).

If you don't have a meat thermometer, check the weight of the roast and cook it for about 17 minutes per pound for rare, 20 minutes per pound for medium, or 26 to 30 minutes per pound for well done.

YORKSHIRE PUDDING

During the year, I taught seven subjects at the Ingersoll Collegiate. I boarded with Mom Swallow, who came from near Leeds in Yorkshire. I went home to Kitchener every Friday night, but usually returned in time to have Mom's Sunday roast beef dinner with Yorkshire pudding served in the proper Yorkshire way—before the meat and potatoes on individual plates.

> **About ¼ cup beef drippings from the roast**
> **2 eggs, slightly beaten**
> **1 cup milk**
> **1 cup flour**
> **½ teaspoon salt**

Mom beat the eggs and milk, then sifted the flour and salt into the mixture. She stirred the ingredients, then let the mixture stand for about 30 minutes. She turned the oven up to 450°F, poured some of the beef drippings from the roast into a shallow baking pan, put the pan in the hot oven till the drippings were bubbling. Then she poured the pudding mixture into the sizzling pan, baked it for 10 minutes, reduced the heat to 350°F, and baked it for 15 to 20 minutes longer—until the pudding was golden and puffed up "with a top and bottom and nothing in t' middle", as J.B. Priestly wrote.

Meanwhile, the family and I were sitting at the dining-room table salivating till Mom rushed in the heated plates with squares of Yorkshire pudding smothered with fabulous brown gravy.

I haven't had anything as good since.

Mother's Pot-Roast

All my cooking life I've been trying to make a pot-roast like my mother's; though she told me many times exactly how she did it, I've never achieved the wonderful flavour she did, nor have my sisters, though Ruby comes closest.

Mother got her butcher to send her "a nice piece of beef"; he knew the kind, she said, not too fat, and no gristle, or bone. Then, contrary to all the rules of meat cookery, she put the meat in a heavy pot with cold water that came about half-way up the sides of the roast. She let it boil slowly, lifting the lid and looking at it, turning it over, adding more boiling water if she thought it necessary. Somewhere along the way she put in a few whole onions. When the meat was tender and the water had almost boiled away, she took the lid off the pot, dropped in two or three bay leaves, and watched the meat constantly, turning it carefully to brown it on all sides in the fatty brown juices (while potatoes and vegetables were cooking separately). When all was ready she put the meat on a platter with the browned onions around it, poured off any excess fat from the pan, and made the most fabulous natural brown gravy that anyone has ever eaten.

BROWN GRAVY

Don't bother reading this if you make good brown gravy; I add nothing new. Blend **4 tablespoons of flour** or **2 of flour and 2 of cornstarch** with cold water in a cup. Pour all the fat you can from the roasting pan into a dish in which you can keep it for later use. Put the roasting pan on the hottest burner of your stove and brown the drippings. Pour in **2½ cups of boiling water**; dissolve, stir, and scrape all the brown from the bottom and sides of the pan. Slowly, stirring the broth as you do it, pour the flour-water mixture into the pan and keep stirring till it thickens. Taste to make sure there is enough salt.

EASY OVEN POT-ROAST

Wrapped in foil with dehydrated onion soup: if you've made this as many hundreds of times as I have, you won't mind if I mention it here for those few who may never have tried this deliciously tender method. It's an especially good way to use a roast you suspect has been in your freezer too long.

Spread out a big piece of heavy foil. Sprinkle **½ a package of onion soup** in the centre and put the **roast** on top. Pat the sides with some of the mix; spread the rest on top. Wrap the roast carefully to seal it in. Put the whole package in a heavy covered pot. Bake at 300°F. You can forget about it for about 3 hours or more, depending on the size of your roast (calculate 30 minutes per pound). After the first hour you'll smell it and salivate. All the juices will be sealed in, and the meat will be gorgeously tender and permeated with flavour. Unwrap the foil. Put the roast on a hot platter surrounded by the brown juices that can be spooned over the meat as you serve it, or scrape the brown juices into the cooking pot and pour in enough boiling water to make gravy thickened with flour. Most of my frozen, cheap-cut pot-roasts have this glorious end.

LENDENBRATEN (Sirloin Roast)

Wait till you taste the thick, rich gravy that comes with this roast.

3 to 4 pound sirloin roast
Salt and pepper
¼ cup butter
1 onion, sliced
1 tomato, sliced
½ cup boiling water
2 tablespoons flour
1 cup sour cream
½ cup white wine (optional)

Season the roast with salt and pepper; brown on all sides in the butter. Slightly brown the onion at the same time, or remove the meat temporarily till you brown it. Put the meat, onion, and tomato in the pan, add boiling water, and put the pan in a 400°F oven for about 30 to 40 minutes, basting frequently. Remove the meat from the pan when it has reached the desired rareness or doneness. To the drippings add flour blended with sour cream and wine. Cook together briefly till the gravy is thickened. Slice the roast and pour the sauce over the servings.

SAUERBRATEN (Sour Beef Pot-Roast)

In 1905 when Prince Louis von Battenburg, vice-admiral of the British Fleet, visited Berlin (now Kitchener), Ontario, the prince particularly relished the sauerbraten served to him at the Berlin Club. It is still a local specialty.

4 pounds beef—chuck, rump, or round
Salt and pepper
3 cups vinegar (I prefer dry red wine)
3 cups water
5 onions, sliced
3 bay leaves
¼ cup brown sugar
4 whole cloves
2 tablespoons dripping or butter
Flour for dredging
½ cup raisins
¼ teaspoon ginger
¼ teaspoon allspice
3 tablespoons flour

Rub the beef with salt and pepper. Place it in a large earthenware dish. Heat the vinegar (or wine), water, onions, bay leaves, sugar, and cloves together, but do not boil. Pour the heated mixture over the beef. Cool, then cover tightly and let stand in a cool place for 3 to 5 days, turning the meat over every day.

Then melt the dripping in a heavy pot; dredge the beef with flour and sear it quickly in the hot fat, turning it to brown on all sides. Pour over the beef the mixture in which it had been standing, diluting a little with water if it seems too sour. Reduce heat, cover the pot, simmer for 2 or 3 hours until the meat is tender and the sour mixture fairly well reduced. Remove the beef and keep it warm. Strain the liquid, skim off the fat, and return the liquid (about 3 or 4 cups) to the pot. Add the raisins, then the spices and flour blended in ½ cup of water; cook until thick and smooth and pour hot over the sliced meat.

POT-ROAST ON RICE
WITH VEGETABLES AND HERBS

Agnes Horst says, "I like a dinner where I can have the whole kaboodle in the oven ahead of time so I can do my quilt-patching till the last minute."

1 tablespoon flour
1 teaspoon salt
¼ teaspoon pepper
1½ teaspoons mixed crumbled herbs (marjoram, basil, thyme)
4 to 5 pound pot-roast
Drippings or suet
2 or more onions, sliced thin
1 carrot per person, sliced
1 stalk celery, sliced
½ cup peas or cut up green beans
Green pepper, sliced (optional)
1 cup uncooked brown rice
2 cups boiling water or bouillon

Mix together the flour, salt, pepper, and 1 teaspoon of the herbs; rub thoroughly into the cut surfaces and sides of the meat. Heat the drippings or suet in a frying-pan and sear all the surfaces of the meat, turning carefully so you don't let out the juices. In a deep roasting pan or clay baker, spread the sliced vegetables and the rice mixed with the remaining ½ teaspoon herbs. Pour in the boiling water and put the seared roast on top, settling it into the rice to get the lid to fit tightly. Put it in a 300°F oven and bake for 2 to 4 hours, adding more boiling water if necessary. The roast should be tender and tasty. A green salad completes the meal.

BRAISED DILL RIBS WITH CARROT GRAVY

Carol Dawson, the pretty sister of the Hutton twins, also used to come to our house every day; now she has a husband, Paul, and three little Dawsons, for whom she likes to cook this delicious Dutch oven meal, which can be easily expanded for company.

Short ribs (however many you need)
2 tablespoons vegetable oil
1 cup water
1 onion, chopped
1 cup grated carrots
2 tablespoons cider vinegar
1 tablespoon salt
¼ teaspoon pepper
1 teaspoon dill seed
½ pound wide noodles
1 tablespoon butter
2 tablespoons flour

Brown the ribs on all sides in the oil and pour off the fat. Put all the ribs in a Dutch oven or heavy pot, add water, onion, carrots, vinegar, salt, and pepper. Cover and simmer over low heat for 2 to 2½ hours till the meat is fork-tender. During the last hour of cooking, add the dill seed. Boil the noodles in salted water, drain, and stir in the butter. Arrange the noodles on a platter with ribs on top and keep them warm. Skim the fat from the mixture in the Dutch oven, blend the flour with some water, and stir into the mixture to make gravy, stirring until it thickens. Pour over the noodles or serve from a gravy bowl.

BRAISED BRISKET

My old friend Pop Swallow often said, "The tastiest part of the cow is the brisket." Layers of lean and fat give it a great flavour. Short ribs are almost as good. Get your butcher to saw the bones in 3-inch lengths. You'll need about 4 pounds for 4 people.

4 pounds brisket or short ribs
¼ cup flour
2½ teaspoons salt
Black pepper
½ teaspoon rosemary or thyme, finely crumbled
1 or 2 onions, chopped
1 stalk of celery, chopped
2 tablespoons beef or bacon drippings
4 to 6 carrots, cut in pieces
1½ cups boiling beef broth or consommé

Dredge the brisket or ribs with the combined flour, seasonings, and herbs. Lightly cook the onion and celery in the drippings, then remove to a heavy pot or casserole with a lid. Brown the ribs on all sides in the same fat. Put the ribs in the pot with the vegetables, add the boiling broth, and cover tightly. Bake in a 300°F oven for 2 or 3 hours, skimming off excess fat before thickening the juices by stirring in the seasoned flour (left from the dredging) mixed with cold water. Simmer till it thickens and serve with the meat and vegetables.

RUNDLES CARBONNADE OF BEEF

John Walker, the *chef de cuisine* of Rundles Restaurant in Stratford, where I took his Stylish Entertainment course, prepared this in no time, while we watched him. Best of all we ate it later with vegetables and fresh Irish Soda Bread. John told us some of the best French dishes are the simplest.

1 pound lean beef
1 bottle lager beer
Salt and pepper
3 or 4 tablespoons flour
2 tablespoons dripping or lard
1 cup onion, finely sliced
2 tablespoons sugar

Cut the meat into half-inch slices; no thinner or they'll disappear. Marinate the meat in the beer overnight or for several hours. Strain off the beer, but keep it, and season the beef with salt and pepper. Pass it through the flour and sear it in hot dripping. Use tongs to place it in a casserole. Don't sear all the meat at one time; pay attention to each piece. Sauté the onions in the hot fat. Spread them over the meat in the baking dish, pour in the beer and the sugar, cover with a tight-fitting lid, and simmer gently in a moderate oven at 350°F for about 2 hours. Put the casserole on a tray to catch any boiling over.

If you've kept a piece of beef in your freezer longer than you should have, make a thick, savoury gravy to give it more flavour.

If you don't have a timer on your oven to warn you to look after what's in there, use an alarm clock.

GRILLED CUTLETS, CHOPS OR STEAKS

At Rundles Restaurant in Stratford you'll be served the best cutlets you've ever eaten. John Walker, the *chef de cuisine*, seasons half-inch **cutlets** with **salt** and **pepper** from a pepper mill, he brushes them lightly on both sides with **oil or melted fat**, places them on the greased bars of the grill, not too close to high heat, and lets them cook and brown for five minutes before turning them with tongs to do the same on the other side. John says about any cutlets, chops, or steaks.

"Once you start cooking them, keep your hands off, don't fidget, don't turn till one side is done. Give the poor things a chance; you're not letting the meat cook if you keep turning it." (The same advice applies to barbecuing.)

John serves his cutlets, chops, or steaks on very hot plates with quarter-inch slices of parsley, herb or garlic butter melting over them. And that really flavours them.

John Walker blends butter with various seasonings to give zest to meats, fish, vegetables, and breads: he blends, shapes, wraps, labels, freezes, and slices the seasoned butter as he needs it.

SWISS STEAK

The smell of this cooking, when we came home from school, gave us a thrill.

Sprinkle a **one-and-a-half-inch-thick round steak** with **salt** and **pepper**, dredge with **flour** on both sides, then pound it well with a wooden potato masher or the edge of a heavy old plate; keep dredging and pounding till the steak won't absorb any more flour. Melt two tablespoons of **beef dripping** in a large iron frying-pan; when it is hot, put the steak in and brown it on both sides. Now cover the steak with **slices of onion** and pour in enough **boiling water** to cover the steak—careful, it will spit. Cover tightly and simmer for one and a half hours. You may occasionally have to add more boiling water. Serve it with boiled or riced potatoes. The gravy is wonderful, and you won't need a steak knife to cut the meat, it can be cut easily with a dull fork.

Bevvy's Meats

Bevvy cooks all her meats and vegetables without consulting a guide, and their flavour is magnificent. She makes potpies of pigeons, rabbits, and veal. She roasts beef, pork, and lamb. Her gravies are brown and shiny. She fries in butter both chickens and, dipped in egg and breadcrumbs, the little fish that her son Amsey catches in the river. She cooks sauerkraut with succulent spareribs. In an iron pot she makes stew and pot-roasts browned with onions and bay leaves. Sometimes she has duck or roast goose bursting with savoury dressing.

BEVVY'S GESCHUTUFFTE STEAK (Stuffed Steak)

Mother made this too, and called it Mock Duck.

2 pounds flank steak
1 onion, minced
3 tablespoons dripping or butter
2 cups bread crumbs
1 stalk of celery, cut fine
2 teaspoons parsley, chopped
½ cup milk
Pinch of freshly crushed sage
Salt and pepper
Flour for dredging
2 onions, sliced
1 cup boiling water
1 cup sour cream (optional)

Lay the steak on a board and pound it. Cook the minced onion in one tablespoon of the dripping, add breadcrumbs, celery, parsley, milk, and seasonings. Spread the mixture over the steak. Roll it up like a jelly roll and tie it with string so it looks like a little body. Dredge the body with flour, then brown it all round in the 2 remaining tablespoons of dripping. Cover it with the sliced onions, pour boiling water into the pan, cover tightly and simmer for two and a half to three hours. Or bake it in a tightly covered roaster at 350°F for two hours. When the body is tender and brown, a cup of sour cream may be added to make marvellous gravy.

Dinner at Eva's

When I was invited to Eva's for a dinner one late autumn Sunday, at noon her children were nowhere to be seen. "I fed them first," Eva told me. "They're playing or reading in their bedrooms upstairs."

The Old Order Mennonite men, wearing their black Sunday suits with the cut-away coats buttoned straight up the front to a neckband, sat on the backless bench between the long kitchen table and the wall. The women, in their plain, printed dresses, aprons, and dainty organdy bonnets tied under their chins with black ribbons, sat on bare, wooden chairs across from the men. Eva's husband and little Harvey sat at one end of the table, her mother and sister at the other end. Eva hovered over us, passing and refilling dishes of potatoes, vegetables, bread, several salads, cheese, browned pork sausage, and gravy beef.

When we had cleared our plates to be ready for the dessert, Hannah helped Eva remove all the empty serving dishes and replaced them with bowls of fruit, pie, cookies, chocolate chiffon cake, butterscotch pudding, and cupfuls of coffee and tea.

We ate until we could eat no more. Then the men moved away to sit on the chairs round the living-room, and the women cleared the table and washed all the dishes before sitting in the room with the men. Soon Eva and Hannah came with bowls full of buttered popcorn, glasses of fruit juice, red shiny apples, luscious squares and homemade fudge, maple cream, and toffee.

Conversation was jolly and interesting until about 4:30 P.M., when the men left to hitch up their horses for the ride home, where chores had to be done before supper.

GRAVY BEEF

When I asked Eva and Hannah for the recipe for this truly delicious meat dish, they looked at each other and both said, "We don't have a recipe. We just make it."

They told me they cut **round steak** into ¾ inch cubes and pack the pieces into sterilized jars with some **salt**—an unspecified amount but just enough for flavouring. They fill the jars and then seal and steam them for three hours before they are cooled and stored on the shelves that line a room in their cellars.

When they need meat for dinner, they empty a jar into a heavy pot, adding enough water to cover it, and put it on the back of the cookstove, where it can simmer gently until it is brown and tender enough to be eaten by even the old and toothless. Sometimes the gravy is thickened with flour, but often it is simply allowed to boil down enough to be put on the platter with the meat, passed round the table, and spooned over mashed potatoes on each waiting plate.

CORNED BEEF

While my dermatologist, Dr. D.J. Grant, was removing a blemish from the bridge of my nose, he talked with great enthusiasm about his way of preparing corned beef. Though his office was filled with waiting patients, he sat down and wrote out the recipe for me.

Put a nice piece of **brisket** into an enamel or earthenware pot with enough water to cover it (so you'll know how much water you need). Remove the brisket temporarily and into the water stir:

2 tablespoons saltpetre
⅓ cup salt
½ a bud (5 cloves) of garlic
2 tablespoons mixed pickling spice

Drop the brisket back into the mixture, cover it, and put it into your fridge for 11 days, turning it over every day. Then discard the marinade, put enough fresh water to cover the brisket into a cooking pot and simmer it for about 4 hours, till it is deliciously tender. If you want to add cabbage during the last 30 minutes of cooking, Dr. Grant told me, that's good, too.

Peter, Barbie, and Agnes

When Peter and my niece Barbie, with their children Kennie and Patti, went to live in the fantastic six-level house that Peter built on a hilltop in the country, they wanted to do all the things they couldn't do in the city. They bred rabbits, kept chickens, two ducks, guinea hens, beehives, a cat that had kittens, a dog, and a budgie. One day Peter went to an auction sale and came home with a cow named Agnes.

When he bid on Agnes, Peter wasn't told that she was the second-wildest of the herd of 150 cattle being auctioned, and that she was pregnant with her fourth calf.

They kept Agnes in the garage and Barbie tried to make friends with her by offering her fragrant, fresh grass; Agnes bunted Barbie and threw her six feet in the air. Barbie didn't try again to win Agnes' affection. She told me, "All we wanted was a gentle family cow and we got this wild animal that won't let us love her."

Peter built a shed for Agnes in the field they could see from the house. There she produced Curly, a stalky, white bull calf. No one dared go near the field where Agnes was grazing.

One night Agnes broke through the fence. With Curly following, she crossed the road and ran down to the Wagner's farm, where she kept circling the house and the barn till Peter and Elmer Wagner finally cornered her. Next day a truck came and took Agnes away to the butcher.

Barbie didn't mind the neat packages that came back to be put in the freezer, but Agnes' unwrapped liver, tongue, and heart, placed on the kitchen counter, gave her more than a shiver. She said, "How can I cook something so personal belonging to our own cow?"

All winter Peter, Barbie, Kennie, and Patti ate Agnes. There seemed to be so much of her. Barbie kept asking for recipes for tough beef; she explained, "Agnes is at her best in a stew."

A year later they were still eating Agnes. Though most of her place in the freezer was taken by Curly, there was still some of Agnes; Barbie said, "We finally just ground her up."

AGNES-AT-HER-BEST

Barbie could put this stew in her oven, run Kennie into town for his music lesson, and drive home to find Agnes simmering gently, tender at last.

> **2 pounds stewing beef**
> **¼ cup flour**
> **¼ teaspoon each thyme, basil, celery seed**
> **⅛ teaspoon sage**
> **1¼ teaspoons salt**
> **Pinch pepper**
> **4 onions, sliced**
> **6 potatoes, thinly sliced or chunked**
> **2 to 4 carrots, sliced**
> **1½ cups hot water**
> **2 bouillon cubes or equivalent**
> **1 teaspoon Worcestershire sauce**
> **¼ cup dry wine**

Dredge the pieces of meat in the flour mixed with herbs and seasonings. In a roasting pan or casserole with a tight lid, put layers of vegetables and meat, sprinkle on the seasoned flour left from the dredging, and pour in the blended liquids. Cover tightly and bake at 325°F for 3 or 4 hours.

Barbie says if you don't like herbs you can omit them, but they seemed to suit Agnes.

MARGARET LAURENCE'S STEW

Whenever I spent a weekend with Margaret, she would have a big pot of stew ready to eat, so she wouldn't have to spend time in the kitchen, instead of sitting and talking.

> **1 or 2 pounds of stewing beef, cut into bite size**
> **pieces**
> **Couple of onions or some green onions**
> **Some carrots**
> **Few potatoes cut in half**
> **Some celery, cut in pieces**

Mixed herbs
Shot of Worcestershire sauce
Enough tomato juice or V-8 juice to come to the
    top of the vegetables.
Mushrooms (optional)

Margaret browned the beef in a pot, added all the rest, and let it cook until it was ready to eat. Sometimes, she put it into the oven at 350°F for a couple of hours. We ate it from bowls with spoons. I wish I could have recorded Margaret's conversation as we ate.

HAMBURGERS WITH GRAVY

In winter when the charcoal grill on the patio has become a bird-feeding station, there's something to be said for the old-fashioned hamburgers Mother used to make for dinner, with gravy, potatoes and a sour cream salad.

1 cup bread or cracker crumbs
½ cup milk
1½ pounds ground beef
1 egg, slightly beaten
1 onion, chopped very finely
Salt and pepper

Soak half the bread crumbs in milk then mix with the remaining ingredients and shape into round, fat patties. Coat the patties with the remaining crumbs and fry in hot beef dripping or butter till browned. Then make gravy (see page 4)—you can't do that on the patio.

MEAT LOAF

I'm not fussy about the kind of beef I use for a meat loaf. I take advantage of the ground-beef specials (if they don't have too much fat), and sometimes, for a change of taste, I put in half a pound of farmers' pork-sausage meat. With baked potatoes and vegetables meat loaf makes a good, easy meal.

**Ground beef (1½ pounds nicely fills my 9 x 5 x 3
   pyrex loaf pan)
2 eggs
½ cup fine bread or cracker crumbs
1 onion, finely sliced
½ stalk celery, chopped
2 tablespoons parsley, chopped
¼ cup milk
2 tablespoons catsup
Squirt of Worcestershire sauce
4 sage leaves, crumbled
Salt and pepper**

Mix everything, pack it into a loaf pan, and bake it in a 325°F oven for 1½ hours. Sometimes I put about ¼ inch of water on top of the loaf so it won't brown too quickly; or I put strips of bacon across the top for the last half hour.

STUFFED MEAT LOAF

To stretch a meat loaf, you can stuff it. Line the bottom and sides of a loaf pan with half of the meat prepared for meat loaf, put in **bread dressing** made with three slices of bread, cover with the remaining meat, and bake in a 325°F oven for about 1½ hours.

It tastes good cold too—if it lasts that long.

TONGUE, HEART, AND LIVER

BEEF TONGUE

Beef tongue is probably the most delicate, tender, economical part of the animal. There is no waste except the skin, which your dog might enjoy. You can make soup of the stock, serve the tongue hot or cold, with vegetables, or a sauce. Mother used to pickle a tongue every Christmas time. My friend Connie sliced hers and set it in tomato aspic. I'm content to eat it with vegetables cooked in the broth.

Put a **tongue** in enough water to cover, season it with **salt**, **pepper**, and whatever else you like, but if you use the broth for soup later you must be discreet. When the tongue has simmered long enough to be tender, a couple of hours, take it out of the stock and peel it. The skin comes off easily. (Give it to your dog before it dries and turns hard.)

Slice the tongue as thick or thin as you like and serve it hot or cold. Try it sometime with Raisin Sauce (page 85).

PICKLED BEEF TONGUE

Mother always made this between Christmas and New Year's as an antidote to all the sweet things we ate too many of.

She boiled a **beef tongue** in **salted water** till it was tender, peeled it, and removed all the ugly little valves and fatty bits on the bottom side. She cut it in thin, even slices, which she put neatly with alternating layers of raw, **thinly sliced onion** into an earthenware dish. Over the meat, and enough to cover, she poured a mixture of **vinegar, sugar**, and **tongue broth** that suited her taste—fairly sour. The slices of tongue were served cold on a plate and any left over were returned to the marinade, where they could be kept for a week.

A cured tongue, which stays red after cooking, looks nicer and will keep longer.

STUFFED HEART

Delicate and different, this is an easy, one-dish oven dinner. One heart should serve 3 or 4 people.

1 beef heart
Salt, pepper and flour for dredging
2 tablespoons beef drippings
1 onion, sliced
2 cups bread crumbs
A few celery leaves, cut up
2 tablespoons parsley, chopped
½ teaspoon crumbled summer savoury (or whatever
is your favourite herb)
1 egg, beaten
Milk
Potatoes, sliced, ½ inch thick
Carrots, sliced
Onions, sliced
Peas or
Green beans
Celery, sliced
Parsley, chopped

Remove the muscles and arteries from the heart. Dredge in salt, pepper, and flour, and brown all around in the beef drippings. Remove the heart from the pan, and in the same fat cook the onion till slightly tender. Turn off the heat, and add bread cubes, celery, parsley, and savoury. Then add egg blended with enough milk to moisten the mixture. Cram the stuffing into the heart, pat it over the top and hope it will stay there—no matter if it doesn't. Put the heart in a casserole with a heavy lid, keeping the stuffing-side up. Pour an inch or two of water into the bottom of the dish and bake the heart in a 325°F oven for a couple of hours until quite tender.

Half an hour before the end of the baking time, add any of the remaining vegetables you want, being sure there is some broth in the pot. Replace the lid and cook till the vegetables are soft enough. Carry the hot dish to the table and enjoy.

LIVER AND BACON

A few strips of crisply fried bacon and calves' liver fried in the bacon fat, just long enough to be not quite pink, is a treat at present astronomical prices.

"We buy beef liver when we see it on sale," Norm and Ralph told me. "We like it just as much as calves' liver, and it's less expensive; we freeze the individual slices so we can take from the freezer whatever we need for a meal." They invited me to the best, liver dinner I've ever eaten; I'll tell you exactly how Norm prepared it.

She put the frozen **liver slices** into hot water (from the tap). "Mother always did that," Norm told me. Then she put the frozen **lean bacon slices** into her electric frying-pan. While the bacon was gently cooking, she peeled and sliced several **onions**. (She works fast.) When the bacon was crisp, she removed it and put the onions into the pan with the bacon fat (not more than 2 tablespoons full). She put the lid on the pan and set it on fairly low heat. Then she drained the liver and dredged it in **flour** mixed with **salt** and **pepper**. When the onions were nicely browned, she shoved them to the side of the pan, and put the bacon strips on top to warm; if there wasn't enough bacon fat left in the pan, she added some butter, then put in the liver slices to cook at medium heat, covered, for about 5 minutes. When the liver was brown on one side, she turned it over and browned it on the other side, uncovered. When it was tender and not quite pink inside, she served it with the bacon and onions, parsley potatoes, and a lettuce salad. She was going to have broccoli, too, but forgot it. And with those golden onions, and liver and bacon, we didn't miss it.

Liver Soufflé

When nutritionists started urging us to eat calves' liver and it became expensive, I decided to try beef liver. A liver soufflé recipe promised to be light and delicious. I baked it in a casserole and proudly brought it to the table, crusty brown and crisp on top. It looked great, until the crust was broken and underneath we discovered a greenish-brown mixture remindful of a newly laid cow flap! Ugh!

We didn't even taste it. But when it cooled, our dear old, white Buddie dog gobbled up every bit.

Veal

I've always enjoyed eating veal, even after my friend Kath Reeves from Devon, refused to eat it because of the cruel way the calves are confined before they are slaughtered. I thought, "Maybe it's that way in England, but not here in Canada." Then one day on the radio I heard someone say that Canadian calves are treated exactly the same way. I haven't bought veal since.

I regret no longer being able to enjoy my mother's veal potpie. I substitute pork in my other veal recipes. Why should I feel less kindly towards pigs? Why do I have no regrets about eating pork? Is it because pigs don't have those soft brown bovine eyes?

Last night on television, I saw an enormous barn full of pigs in stalls so narrow the animals couldn't turn around, because it might toughen their muscles.

I often wish I had the guts to be consistent and become a vegetarian.

VEAL POTPIE

In Mexico a few years ago, I stayed at a gourmet's paradise, el Casa de Piedra in Cuernavaca. Every day wealthy Mexicans would drive 70 miles from Mexico City to have dinner there, Americans from neighbouring hotels came for a meal, movie stars and visiting celebrities dropped in to eat. For two weeks we dined on the kind of food I like to read about when I'm lonely: avocados stuffed with strawberry shrimp, crêpes flambées marquise, coq au vin, Milanesas with mushroom béchamel, bouillabaisse, artichoke mousse, soufflé pate de foie gras. Every dish was a work of art produced by the owner of the casa, a Spanish marquesa whose hobby was cooking.

After two weeks of savouring and delighting in her culinary surprises, I suddenly couldn't face any more of them. I looked at my Lobster Costa Brava without any zest. I said to my companion, "I'd give anything right now for something really simple, like veal potpie the way Mother makes it at home."

Like this: She'd cut a pound or so of **veal** into pieces and slightly brown them in 3 tablespoons of **butter**, then pour enough **boil-**

ing water over the veal to cover it entirely. When the veal was nice and tender, she'd drop **Egg Dumplings** (see page 86) into the pot, cover it tightly for 15 minutes till the dumplings were cooked, then thicken the broth and add lots of cut-up **parsley**. Sometimes, when I make veal potpie I cook potatoes, carrots, onions, and peas along with the veal, but mostly I like the bland flavour of the unadulterated veal and dumplings best of all.

DANUTA'S VEAL CUTLETS

Danuta has learned many delicious and unusual Polish dishes from her mother.

> **1 pound veal (or pork) cutlets**
> **½ cup flour**
> **1 teaspoon basil, chopped**
> **1 teaspoon salt**
> **Pepper**
> **¼ cup cooking oil**
> **¼ cup dry wine**
> **¼ cup honey**
> **2 tablespoons cooking oil**
> **½ cup onion, sliced**
> **¼ cup raisins**
> **3 tablespoons parsley, chopped**
> **1 tablespoon wine vinegar**
> **1 teaspoon paprika**
> **1 teaspoon celery seed**
> **½ teaspoon salt**

Pound the cutlets until they are thin. Combine the flour with the basil, salt, and pepper; dredge the cutlets in the mixture. Heat a ¼ cup of oil in a skillet and brown the cutlets quickly on both sides over high heat. Reduce the heat to low and fry about 10 minutes on each side, or until the veal is cooked. Meanwhile, combine all the remaining ingredients in a saucepan and bring to a boil. Simmer for 5 to 10 minutes, then pour over the browned cutlets. Serve with rice or noodles and vegetables of your choice.

WIENER SCHNITZEL

The first time I ordered this in a restaurant in Germany, I was surprised when I didn't get wieners. Mother always called this Breaded Veal Cutlet.

2 pounds veal steak, ½ inch thick
Salt and pepper
½ cup milk
1 cup fine bread or cracker crumbs
2 eggs, beaten
Drippings or butter
¼ cup boiling water
Chopped parsley
Lemon slices

Cut the veal steak into serving pieces. Sprinkle with salt and pepper, dip in milk, then in crumbs, then in egg, and again in crumbs. Heat the drippings or butter and brown the veal on both sides till it is golden—not too quickly. Turn down the heat. Pour in the boiling water and simmer, covered, for 10 minutes; uncover and brown again. Sprinkle with parsley and serve, letting your eaters sprinkle the veal with lemon juice if they care to.

Planning Menus

When you invite the Smiths or the Joneses for a meal, be sure you haven't given them the same menu four or five times, unless they have told you they simply adore your pigs' tails and sauerkraut and hope you'll keep having them again and again.

Do you enjoy a reputation of being a one-meal cook? Maybe, but not likely. When you've had a dinner party or luncheon and you've made a meal you were proud of, write in a little notebook the date, who your guests were, the menu, and a few notes. When you have other friends in, you can repeat your success.

Keep trying different dishes until you have a number of menus you know you are good at. You'll soon enjoy your reputation for being a wonderful cook.

Don't be disturbed if a company meal is not quite ready when your guests are. If they are kept waiting, they'll be really hungry and they'll think everything you serve them is marvellous.

TZVIVELLE SCHNITZEL

Onions and sour cream give this veal steak more flavour.

2 pounds veal steak, 1 or 1½ inches thick
Salt and pepper
Flour
1 cup sliced onions
½ cup boiling water
¾ cup sour cream

Cut the steak into serving pieces, sprinkle with salt and pepper, and roll in flour. Melt drippings in a heavy frying-pan, add the onions, and cook gently for about 5 minutes. Push the onions aside, put in the meat, and brown it lightly on both sides. Pour in the boiling water and cover tightly; simmer for 30 minutes, turning the meat once. Add the sour cream, cover again, and simmer another 15 minutes or until the meat is tender. The gravy this makes is divine.

Rabbit

I've always liked cottontail bunnies hopping around in the grass, and the bold one who come to my patio to eat sunflower seeds with the cardinals. But right now, after seeing all winter how the rabbits have been nibbling the bark off my new little trees, I wouldn't mind trying a few rabbit recipes.

RABBIT PIE

This is wonderful on a cold winter's night, while the other rabbits are out there on the lawn nibbling the bark off your trees.

> **1 rabbit (though a dozen would be better)**
> **Salt**
> **3 tablespoons butter**
> **2 tablespoons chopped onion**
> **1½ tablespoons flour for**
>   **each cup of liquid**
> **Pepper**
> **2 tablespoons parsley**
> **Pastry crust**

Cut the rabbit into pieces, place in a saucepan, and barely cover with water. Cover the pan and simmer until the meat is tender, adding salt half-way through the cooking. Drain and measure the broth. Remove the meat from the bones, keeping it in large pieces. Heat the butter in a frying-pan, add onion, and cook about 5 minutes, stirring constantly. Pour the broth into the pan and thicken with the flour. Add pepper and parsley. Put the rabbit meat into the sauce, then pour the whole mixture into a greased baking dish. Cover with a pastry top and bake in a 350°F oven for 35 minutes, till the crust is golden. No one will know this isn't chicken.

In Neil's Harbour, Cape Breton, they always had Rabbit Pie on Christmas Eve after the service in the little wooden church on the edge of the sea.

FRIED RABBIT

If you have a hunter in your family, here is a way to please him or her with very little effort.

After the **rabbit** has been skinned and cleaned, and cut in pieces (let the hunter do it), soak in **salt water** overnight. Remove it from the water, drain it, and roll it in **flour**. In a hot frying-pan melt about ¼ **cup** of **lard and butter;** put the rabbit pieces in, cover, and fry slowly to a golden brown, turning often. Season with **salt** and **pepper**, add **1 cup of boiling water**, cover and simmer till the rabbit is tender. Take the rabbit from the pan and make rabbit gravy.

HASENPFEFFER

This is the deluxe way to cook rabbit.

> **1 or 2 cut-up rabbits**
> **3 cups dry wine or vinegar**
> **3 cups water**
> **1 large onion, sliced**
> **Salt and pepper**
> **½ teaspoon ginger**
> **1 teaspoon whole cloves**
> **4 bay leaves**
> **2 slices of lemon**
> **Flour**
> **Fat for frying**
> **1 cup thick sour cream**

Put the rabbit pieces in a large bowl or crock, and cover with wine and water. Add the onion and seasonings. Let the meat soak in this solution for two days. On the third day put the rabbit in a kettle. (Save the solution.) Cover the rabbit with water, adding the lemon slices to keep the flesh white. Boil until the meat is tender, about an hour, and remove from the kettle. Dip the pieces of rabbit lightly in flour and fry in hot fat in a frying-pan, browning quickly, turning often. Gradually add some of the mixture in which the meat was pickled. Let simmer until the broth is brown, about 30 minutes. Just before serving, stir sour cream into the sauce.

Lamb

When my sisters and I went on a tour of New Zealand, we especially liked watching the country's 73 million sheep, dotting the green meadows being herded by the well-trained sheep dogs. We ordered and enjoyed eating lamb at dinner every single day. We were told the most flavourful was not the dear little milk-fed baby lambs (thank goodness), but one-year-old hogget, which, six months later, would be called mutton and have a stronger taste. Of course, nothing we ate was ever called mutton on a hotel or restaurant menu. I don't think in my entire long life I have been told I was eating mutton.

ROAST LEG OF LAMB

I always buy a 5-pound leg of lamb trimmed of fat. I used to roast it as I would a roast of beef—sprinkled with salt, in a 350°F oven until the meat thermometer stuck in the centre reached 170°F for well done. After I ate roast lamb at the home of Ian Sclanders, who was then articles editor of *Maclean's* magazine, I have roasted my legs of lamb as he told me he did his.

Ian cut small slits in the skin of the **leg of lamb** with a pointed knife, and in each he inserted a **slice of a garlic clove**; then he rubbed the meat with **rosemary** blended with **lemon juice**, and sprinkled it with **salt** and **pepper**. He roasted it at 350°F, un-covered, for about 15 minutes to the pound for medium-well done lamb. Served with mint sauce or jelly, and new potatoes with pan gravy, and fresh garden peas, it was a feast. I would never roast a leg of lamb any other way.

LAMB STEW

Always the Lamb-in-a-Basket had several **odd bits and pieces of meat** that I wasn't sure what to do with. A stew could never go wrong. I browned the meat on all sides in **butter**, then sprin-kled it with **salt, pepper**, and **flour**, put it in a heavy pot, added enough **water** to almost cover it, brought it to a boil, then simmered it, covered, for an hour or so till the meat was almost tender. Then I added whatever **vegetables** I had to make a good brew. When they too were tender, we had an easy, filling meal.

Broiled Lamb Chops or Cutlets

*At one time the supermarkets sold what they called
"Lamb-in-a-Basket." It was quite a large pack of various
cuts and was fairly inexpensive. It gave thrifty shoppers,
like me, a chance to experiment.*

*There were never enough lamb chops in the basket; if I
needed them I always bought more, allowing at least three
per person. I broiled them as I was taught by John Walker
in Rundles' Stylish Entertainment course. No wonder there
was never enough.*

BRAISED LAMB

Sometimes I braised those undetermined **lamb pieces**—they
might have been shoulder. They were usually bony, and we
could eat them with our fingers, when we didn't have company
to criticize our bad manners.

I dredged the pieces in **flour, salt, pepper**, and **basil**, then
browned them in **oil**. Then with **1 cup of water**, a shot of **red
wine**, and a couple of **garlic cloves**, I put them in a pan and
baked them, covered, in a 350°F oven until the meat was tender,
about 1½ hours or less.

BAKED LAMB SHANKS

There were never any lamb shanks in the basket, but they are
a very convenient buy if you don't need as much as a leg of lamb.
Try one shank per person, unless you know someone might eat
two. Dredge the **lamb shanks** in **flour** seasoned with **salt,
pepper**, and your preference of **herbs**. Brown them all round in
oil, then put them in a covered baking dish or casserole, add
whatever cut-up **vegetables** you like (onions, carrots, celery,
green beans, tomato, garlic). Potatoes or turnip should be added
½ an hour before the end, or they get mushy. Pour **1½ cups of
boiling bouillon** or water (or ¾ cup dry red wine and ¾ cup
water) into the pot and bake about 1½ hours, or until the meat
is tender.

If you'd rather not add the vegetables, that's all right with me.

REAL IRISH STEW

In a Dublin hotel dining-room we watched a fashion show of very smart suits made of hand-loomed Donegal tweeds, while we ate real Irish stew. There was no other choice.

1 pound mutton or lamb
½ pound back bacon
1 cup cold water
3 medium onions, sliced
8 potatoes, peeled
1 teaspoon salt
½ teaspoon dry mustard
A good shake of pepper

Trim the fat off the mutton and slice into 1½-inch cubes. Cut the back bacon into pieces. Slightly warm your heavy cooking pot and rub it with a bit of the trimmed mutton fat. Put in the mutton, bacon, and cold water. Bring slowly to a boil, then simmer gently for 1 hour. Add the onions, potatoes, and seasoning. Continue cooking until the potatoes are done. Add more water if required. Serve with green cabbage or Brussels sprouts.

Pork

ROAST PORK

Your roast pork won't be stringy and dry if you cook it the way Mother did hers.

Sprinkle a **5- or 6-pound roast** with **salt** and **pepper** (and a bit of **ginger**); put it in a roasting pan that has a tight lid. Pour about **1 cup of water** into the pan with the meat and bake in a 300°F oven for most of the afternoon—4 or 5 hours. Look in now and then to make sure there is still some liquid in the pan, until the last hour. The meat will become brown with the lid on; if for some reason yours doesn't, turn up the oven to 350°F. During the last hour of roasting, you might put some **onions** into the pot to cook along with the meat and to flavour that delicious brown gravy. On a cold winter's day you might add a can of **sauerkraut**. And don't forget baked potatoes.

ROAST PORK WITH STUFFED APPLES

Apples served round a pork roast aren't much trouble and give it that special touch. Place **cored apples** round the roast about ½ hour before it is finished and bake until the apples are soft.

BREADED PORK TENDERLOIN

In the good old days when pork was a bargain, Mother often bought a piece of **tenderloin**. She'd lay it on a board and pound it with her wooden potato masher till it was stretched and quite flat; then she'd cut it into serving pieces and dip both sides into slightly beaten **egg** and **breadcrumbs**. She'd sprinkle the pieces with **salt** and **pepper**, then gently fry them in **butter** till they were golden brown on both sides and thoroughly cooked throughout.

STUFFED PORK TENDERLOIN

This was a company dish; and knowing how much I enjoyed it, Mother used to send some to me in a box with other goodies when I was away at university—for those midnight chats with the girls.

Mother would flatten the **pork tenderloin** to stretch it as far as she could, then she'd spread a **bread dressing** over it—the same as she used for stuffed steak or Mock Duck (see page 12). She held the edges of the tenderloin together and sewed them with string to enclose the dressing and make a neat, firm little roll. In a covered roasting pan with very little water, she'd bake it in a 300°F oven until it was tender and delicately brown. At home she served it hot, and she made gravy; in our school residence we were happy to have it in neat, cold little slices.

PORK CHOPS

Of course you know there are two kinds of pork chops: rib chops with the bone along the side of the solid meaty part, and loin chops, which are larger, boneless, with bits of fat marbling the slightly darker meat. I prefer loin chops to bake in the oven.

SMOKED PORK CHOPS

These are a gourmet's delight and the quickest of all chops to do because they are pre-processed. Buy them from a German butcher. While your guests are having their last drink, put the chops under the broiler till they are brown round the edges on both sides—about 20 minutes. They are easy to make and easy to serve, too.

FRIED PORK CHOPS

If you want to cook ordinary, raw pork chops in a hurry, you can simply fry them or broil them till they are thoroughly cooked. Mother always fried hers in butter, and I've never had any better.

WITH SCALLOPED POTATOES

Loin chops baked on top of scalloped potatoes till they are very, very tender is one of my favourite ways. Cover them till the last half-hour in a 300°F oven. I always put a pan under the baking dish to catch any milk that might bubble over.

WITH ONIONS AND CONSOMMÉ

Coat loin chops with a mixture of flour, salt, and pepper, put them into a greased casserole on a layer of thinly sliced onions, and over all pour two cups boiling consommé or bouillon. Bake in a 300°F oven for two hours with potatoes baking alongside. During the last hour you might toss in a few other vegetables and herbs.

WITH SOUR CREAM

This is super. Season 4 loin chops cut ½ an inch thick with salt and pepper, dredge them with flour, and brown them in a small amount of fat. Put them into a casserole. Blend and add:

**½ cup water
½ cup sour cream
2 tablespoons wine or vinegar
1 tablespoon brown sugar
1 bay leaf**

Cover and bake in a 350°F oven for 1½ hours or until the chops are done and the baked potatoes, squash, or other vegetables, you've naturally put into the oven at the same time, are tender.

BRINKEY'S SWEET AND SOUR SAUCE FOR PORK CHOPS

Ruby's friend pours this sauce over pork chops; Ruby says it's good on other meats, too.

**½ cup white sugar
½ cup brown sugar
½ can tomato soup, undiluted
¼ cup vinegar, lemon juice, or white wine
Pinch of chili powder**

Blend all ingredients together, pour over chops, and simmer in a 300°F oven till the chops are tender.

MARY ANN MARTIN'S BREADED PORK CHOPS

Prepare these ahead of time and cook them while your guests breathe in their delicious aroma.

4 or 5 lean pork chops
1 cup white vinegar or wine
Flour for dredging
1 egg, slightly beaten
½ cup fine biscuit or breadcrumbs
½ teaspoon salt
Pepper
¼ teaspoon garlic powder
1 teaspoon dried parsley or herbs
1½ tablespoons oil
1½ tablespoons bacon fat or butter

Marinate the chops in the vinegar or wine for an hour at room temperature, or overnight in the fridge, turning several times. Drain and pat dry. Dredge the chops with flour, then dip in the egg, adding a bit of water to the egg if you need it. Combine the crumbs and seasonings. Roll the chops in the crumbs, coating them well on all sides. Let stand a few minutes, or put them in the fridge till you are ready to cook them. Heat the oil in a heavy skillet, adding bacon fat or butter for a better flavour. Put in the chops and brown nicely on both sides. Lower the heat, cover, and cook slowly for about 45 minutes, or cover and put in a slow oven (250°F to 300°F) until tender, adding a bit of water if necessary to prevent sticking. Turn the chops once. Uncover the last 5 minutes of cooking to crisp the neat golden coating.

DOUG GIBSON'S SWEET AND SOUR PORK CHOPS

Besides being the beloved publisher of many of Canada's best-selling authors, Doug Gibson, when he has time, likes to grill pork chops in his own special way.

Doug grills the chops until they are well cooked and until they are brown on both sides. He bastes them with a mixture of maple syrup and lemon juice, but the exact amounts are Doug's own innovation. You might try a combination of your own, with more than satisfactory results.

Oktoberfest

Every year, North America's greatest Bavarian festival attracts more than 600,000 visitors to Kitchener-Waterloo for fun, food, and hospitality. Gemütlichkeit is the spirit, Ein Prosit the theme song. Oktoberfest sausage-on-a-bun is the favourite snack.

For nine days in mid-October, revellers in 30 banner-decorated fest-halls link arms and sing traditional drinking songs. Waiters in lederhosen and waitresses in dirndls serve pitchers of foaming beer. Brassy German bands play oom-pah-pah music for gaily-costumed locals, ethnic dancers, Schuhplattlers, and entertainers from Munich and Austria. Thousands twirl in a polka, then fill up their plates from smorgasbords laden with millions of cabbage rolls, wiener schnitzels, rouladen, spareribs, and pigs' tails, apfelstrudel, and Black Forest cakes prepared by the ladies of service groups and German-Canadian clubs who operate the festhallen and gigantic beer tents.

Besides the merry-making in the beer halls, 70 cultural and general events can be enjoyed. Rooted in centuries-old German traditions, with Kitchener-Waterloo's own innovations, Oktoberfest offers the visitors operetta, symphony, choir concerts, arts and crafts, tours of the Mennonite countryside, bow-and-arrow competitions, barrel-rolling contests, water polo, squash, a schuetzenfest, racquetball, tennis, golf, hockey, a horse show, a polka mass at St. Aloysius church, and brunch at Trinity United Church near Kitchener's famous Farmers' Market. Wherever they are, the visitors exclaim, "Wunderbar!" and munch on Oktoberfest sausage with sauerkraut-on-a-bun.

The American Bus Association has chosen Kitchener-Waterloo's Oktoberfest as the number-one event to visit in Canada. If you can't join the busloads that come from California, Wisconsin, Iowa, Illinois, the Eastern States, and all over Canada, you can celebrate your own Oktoberfest by watching on television the three-mile, hour-and-a-half-long Thanksgiving Day parade, an extravaganza with fabulous floats, marching bands, and clattering brau wagons drawn by magnificent horses.

*And when it's all over, you can serve your own
sauerkraut, schnitzel, sausage or spareribs, apfelstrudel
and Black Forest cake, then refill your beer stein and twirl
off the calories in a polka, oom-pah-pah, oom-pah-pah, and
Ein Prosit.*

MY FAVOURITE CIDER AND HONEY-GLAZED RIBS

In Waterloo Region we have no use for spareribs. We have thick,
meaty ribs, not spare ones. These are easy to prepare and divine
to eat.

2 to 3 strips of ribs (enough for 6)
3 cups cider
½ cup honey
2 tablespoons lemon juice
2 teaspoons sage
1½ teaspoons dry mustard
1 teaspoon thyme
Salt

Spread the ribs in a large shallow pan. Blend all the other
ingredients and pour over the meat. Marinate in a cold place for
several hours or overnight. Turn the ribs occasionally. Take the
ribs from the pan but save the marinade. Spread the ribs in a
large baking pan—the less they overlap the better. Bake at
350°F; set your timer for 20 minutes, then generously baste the
meat with the marinade. Baste every 20 minutes for 1½ hours,
or until the ribs are tender and the marinade has turned into an
irresistible glaze. Of course, ribs should be served with boiled,
mashed, or baked potatoes and sauerkraut, but other vegetables will do.

SHERRY-GLAZED SPARERIBS

So-called "country ribs" are good done this way, so are any meaty ribs. But keep your eye on them. Don't go to the neighbour's for a drink and come home to find the ribs black on the bottom.

2 strips ribs
½ cup sherry
½ cup water
¼ cup brown sugar
3 tablespoons soya sauce
1 tablespoon cornstarch

Cut the ribs into serving pieces and arrange them in a single layer in a shallow baking pan. Combine all remaining ingredients and pour the mixture over the ribs. Bake, covered with foil, at 325°F for about 1 hour and 30 minutes, or until the meat is tender, turning occasionally. Remove the foil for 2 or 3 minutes to brown. Skim off excess fat before serving. If you like to experiment, you could cover the ribs with sliced onions, and instead of the sherry, use a fruit juice or anything else you think might be interesting.

MOTHER'S BAKED SPARERIBS

We always rejoiced when Mother came home from the market with a long, meaty piece of spareribs. She would sprinkle the ribs generously with salt and pepper, stretch them out in a roasting pan, pour in a cup and a half of boiling water, put on the lid and roast in a 350°F oven for an hour and half, longer if the meat was thick. She'd remove the lid and let the ribs brown on both sides.

SCHWEINE SCHWANTZ (Pigs' Tails)

Sticky, browned, succulent pigs' tails are a superlative local specialty; no stag party or office picnic in Kitchener-Waterloo is a success without pigs' tails and rolls of barbecued spareribs prepared by local caterers, but you can make them at home and you will be blessed. Pigs' tails really are the greatest treat of all. Suppose you have 24 or more pigs' tails (never underestimate—they're good warmed over): lay them on a rack in a covered roasting pan and let them roast in a 300°F oven for 3 or 4 hours till most of the fat has baked out. Pour off all the fat and coat the tails all around or dip them in the following sauce:

> 1 cup of tomato sauce
> 1 cup of brown sugar
> ½ cup of tomato paste
> 1 teaspoon of dry mustard
> A shot or two of Worcestershire
>   sauce
> Salt and pepper

Add also whatever you like: a few spoonfuls of prepared barbecue sauce, or soya sauce, or ketchup, hickory smoke salt, and so forth: keep tasting until you think your mixture is marvellous. Put the coated tails, covered, back into the oven at 300°F for another hour or so (if you're impatient try them uncovered at 350°F for 30 minutes) until they are bubbly and a deep, reddish-brown.

Provide your guests with big serviettes, or wet washcloths, because they must hold the tails with their fingers to get all the sweet, sticky skin and meat off the bones. The local caterers always have scalloped potatoes and coleslaw to go with the pigs' tails—and of course plenty of beer. I like baked potatoes and bean salad with mine.

BROWN SUGAR AND BEER GLAZED PORK HOCKS

Pork hocks are usually a bargain and there is no more tender, succulent meat than there is under that glazed brown exterior.

6 pork hocks (one per person)
2 onions
2 cloves garlic
2 teaspoons salt
Pinch of pepper
2 bay leaves
6 cloves
3 tablespoons wine or lemon juice

Glaze:
1 cup brown sugar
2 teaspoons dry mustard
¼ cup drippings from the hocks
½ cup beer or broth

Put the hocks in a kettle with onions, garlic, salt, pepper, bay leaves, cloves, and wine, with enough water to cover the hocks. Bring to a boil, cover, and simmer for about 2 hours, or until the hocks are very tender.

Arrange the hocks in a baking pan, mix together the sugar, mustard, drippings, and enough beer or broth to make a spreading mixture. Coat the hocks all round and broil until crisp, turning them to broil on all sides. Or, simply put in a 400°F oven and let nature take its course, but watch it.

You should serve these with potatoes and sauerkraut.

SAUER SOSSE

Because I didn't like onions or vinegar, I'd turn up my nose when Mother made pickled pigs' feet; the rest of the family thought it was a treat.

4 or 5 pigs' feet
3 cups meat stock
1½ cups vinegar
4 onions, sliced
2 tablespoons salt
1 teaspoon whole cloves (optional)
1 bay leaf

Put the feet in a kettle with enough salted water to cover them; simmer them for about 2 or 3 hours, or until the meat falls from the bones. Skim off the fat. To the meat stock add the vinegar, onions, salt, and spices tied in a bag; simmer about 30 minutes longer. Take out the spices, put the meat in a crockery bowl, and pour the sour liquid and onions over it. Serve hot, or chill until completely cold and the liquid jells; then slice and serve. As I said, this is fine for anyone who likes onions and pigs' feet.

GALLRICH

Jellied pigs' hocks are a Mennonite favourite–not mine.

Cover a couple of **pig's feet or a pig's knuckle** with **salted water** and boil till the meat falls from the bones. Chop up the meat fairly fine, removing the fat and any bits you don't like the look of. Return the meat to the broth, which should by now be reduced to about two or three cupfuls. Put in a couple of **bay leaves**, **pepper**, and any other **flavouring** you like; simmer the mixture for about 15 minutes. Pour it into a loaf pan and set it away to cool and become firm.

HOT HEAD CHEESE

Sometimes Mother would buy a piece of head cheese at the Kitchener market, put it in a pot with ¼ cup of water, and let it heat till it's melted and bubbled; then she'd serve it to us poured over boiled, hot potatoes. With a sour cream salad it was a quick, easy, delectable meal.

It also makes a great meal for a loner. I love it.

SUMMER SAUSAGE

"We don't always have fresh meat in the country," Bevvy says, "but only right after we butcher. We have to cure it to keep it. Some we make into sausage; some we pack solid in jars and steam it. We smoke beef and ham. What we like best is the summer sausage; it is beef and pork ground real fine with seasoning and saltpetre, then stuffed tight in cotton bags the size of a lady's stocking, and smoked for a week with maple smoke."

"We can eat that every day; we never get sick of it," her husband David says.

"We couldn't live without summer sausage", little Amsey says as he slaps a slice on a piece of bread and butter.

"Ach, we could live without, only we rather wouldn't", Bevvy says. "We got all other kinds yet, like liverwurst and head cheese; they're mostly made from the pork scraps, but they go good with fried potatoes and pickles, small corn on the cob, or beet and red-cabbage salad."

I've never made summer sausage; I buy it at the farmers' market, or from Mr. Weber in Yattan, or from Mennonite farmers who have signs on their gate-posts that add, "No Sunday Sales." Here is Bevvy's recipe:

66 pounds beef, ground very fine
33 pounds of side meat, ground
4 pounds salt
½ pound ground pepper
½ pound saltpetre
3 pounds sugar

Mix well, stuff solidly into firm cotton bags, hang from a ceiling in a dry room where they won't freeze for a few days, then smoke with maple smoke for a week, and hang again from the rafters. Summer sausage keeps for months in a dry, cold place.

Neil's Harbour Bologna

When I first visited Neil's Harbour, in Cape Breton, supplies were brought in once a week by the ASPY, a small freight and passenger vessel that called at the villages of Cape Breton's north shore. The boat brought very little fresh meat. Bologna was popular, because a family could buy the exact number of slices that were needed for a meal.

Clara May would nick the edges of the bologna slices so they wouldn't curl. She'd dip them in milk, sprinkle them with salt and pepper, dip them in fine bread crumbs, then into beaten egg, and again in crumbs. She pan-fried the slices in melted dripping, turning them carefully to brown both sides.

With boiled potatoes and turnip, bologna day was special.

Hot Ring Bologna

For emergency meals I keep a ring of bologna in my freezer, and when someone comes unexpectedly for a meal I find it, hammer a knife through it to get the amount I need, put the rest back in the freezer, and heat what I want in my toaster oven. Hot bologna seems to have more flavour and is very tasty served with potatoes and coleslaw, or beet and red cabbage salad.

Ham

The only kinds of hams I've seen in Canadian cities for years have been pink, pre-cooked, delicate, and fool-proof to prepare. They are completely unlike the smoked, dark-red ham my mother used to cook for hours and in several waters to make it less salty; as we ate it someone was sure to say, "This is a good ham, not too strong."

I've had dark-red, smoked ham in an Old Amish–Mennonite farmhouse in North Waterloo County and in Colmar, a charming, mouldy little thirteenth-century

city in southern Alsace, where there is still a Mennonite
meeting house and the ham was served cold, paper-thin,
with crusty French bread, tender leaf-lettuce, and bleached
asparagus dipped in melted butter.

BAKED HAM

I must concede, that if I want to serve a lot of people there's
nothing simpler than a big, modern, tenderized, easily carved
ham, placed fat-side up in the oven at 325°F allowing 16 minutes
per pound if it's over 12 pounds, and 20 minutes per pound if
it's less. About 45 minutes before the end comes, make a paste
of:

> **1 cup brown sugar**
> **¼ cup flour**
> **¼ cup maple syrup**
> **1 teaspoon dry mustard**
> **Cloves**

Remove the rind and some of the fat from the ham, cut the
remaining fat to form diamonds, rub the paste over the ham,
stud it with cloves, and return it to the oven to brown, basting
it occasionally with dribbles of cider or sherry.

GLAZED HAM

Buy the type and size of **ham** you like, put it in a roasting pan
and heat it in a 350°F oven for an hour, unless it is an uncooked
one, then you must bake it 25 minutes to the pound until it is
done. Remove it from the oven and cut off the rind with shears
or a sharp knife. Score the fat diagonally about ⅛ inch deep to
make a diamond pattern. Spread over the ham whichever **glaze**
you prefer. Increase the oven heat to 400°F and return the ham
to the oven until the glaze is browned.

Don't apologize for serving small portions of meat, at today's
prices people are lucky to have meat. Give them more vegetables.

BROWN SUGAR GLAZE WITH CLOVES

A lot of whole cloves
1 cup brown sugar
2 teaspoons dry mustard
A little ham fat

Stud the corners of the diamond pattern with the cloves. Combine the sugar, mustard, and enough ham fat from the roasting pan to make spreading easy. Spread it over the ham, return it to the 400°F oven, and bake until the sugar forms a glaze.

BEER AND BROWN SUGAR GLAZE

1 cup brown sugar
3 tablespoons breadcrumbs
1 teaspoon dry mustard
½ cup beer

Mix the sugar, breadcrumbs, mustard, and enough beer to make a paste that spreads easily over the ham. Return it to a 400°F oven and bake until a glaze is formed.

APPLESAUCE GLAZE

Cloves (optional)
1 cup applesauce
⅔ cup brown sugar
½ teaspoon cinnamon
¼ teaspoon nutmeg
½ cup beer or ham dripping

Stud the ham with cloves. Mix the remaining ingredients together and spread over the ham. Return to the 350°F oven and bake for 30 minutes longer.

SEIFLAISCH UND BOHNA (Ham with Green Beans)

Bevvy makes this when she's having a crowd.

She covers a **ham** with **water** and cooks it slowly for three hours, or until it is tender, adding boiling water from time to time to have at least one quart of broth at all times—more if she has a lot of people to feed. Then into the pot with the ham she puts as many **potatoes**, peeled and cut in quarters, and as many **green string beans**, whole or broken into one-inch pieces, as she thinks she needs. She cooks all together till tender, serves the meat on a platter, and the vegetables in a bowl. With a salad, thick apple sauce, and a couple of sours, her meal is a feast.

SCHNITZ UND KNEPP (Apple Segments and Dumplings)

My gourmet friends from Toronto were enthusiastic about this Mennonite specialty.

> **2 cupfuls of dried schnitz (or peeled, raw apple**
> **segments if you can't get dried)**
> **smoked ham (butt or picnic)**
> **½ cup raisins (optional)**
> **2 tablespoons brown sugar**
> **Egg dumplings (page 86)**

Soak the dried schnitz overnight. Boil the ham for two or three hours in water. Add the dried apples with the water in which they were soaked, or the raw apples, the raisins, and the sugar. Boil together for 15 minutes then drop the stiff dumpling batter by spoonfuls into the boiling broth with the apples and ham. Cover tightly for 15 minutes without lifting the lid.

Ready to eat? Put the ham in the centre of a deep platter, surround it with the apples and a circle of dumplings sprinkled with browned buttered crumbs. Buttered cauliflower, green beans, and red cabbage, and beet salad go well with schnitz und knepp.

GEBROTENE SCHUNKA (Fried Ham)

If somewhere in this world you can find a **¾-inch slice of old-fashioned red ham**, plop it into an inch of boiling water in your iron frying-pan, cover it and cook it gently till the water has boiled away; uncover it, watch it, turn it, and let it fry till it browns a bit on both sides. Serve it with **potatoes** and a **sour-cream salad** of beans, cabbage, dandelion, or endive, and you'll never forget it.

SCHUNKA IN MILLICH (Ham Baked in Milk)

Put this in the oven, go to church, come home, and have it for brunch with scrambled eggs and hot biscuits, or for dinner with vegetables.

1 round slice of ham, 1¼ to 1½ inches thick
¾ teaspoon dry mustard
2 tablespoons brown sugar
Milk to cover

Put the ham in a large iron frying-pan, rub it with dry mustard and sprinkle sugar over it. Pour in enough milk to cover the ham. Bake at 325°F and hope that the preacher doesn't keep you longer than 1½ hours. By then the milk should be absorbed and crusty over the ham.

CRANBERRY-GLAZED BACK BACON

This is one of Kit's favourite company meals. It looks special and tastes even better.

2 pounds back bacon
2 tablespoons butter
½ cup onion, chopped
⅔ cup ketchup, tomato sauce, or chili sauce
1½ cups cranberries
½ cup packed brown sugar
2 tablespoons vinegar
1 teaspoon dry mustard

Bake the bacon on a rack at 375°F for 45 minutes, or until tender. Meanwhile, in a skillet melt the butter. Add the onion and cook until soft, but not brown. Stir in the ketchup, cranberries, brown sugar, vinegar, and mustard. Bring to a boil, then reduce heat and simmer, uncovered, for 15 minutes. Spoon sauce over the bacon and bake for 30 minutes longer, basting a few times.

SAUSAGES

PORK SAUSAGE, PLAIN OR SMOKED

Nothing could be more Waterloo County than sausage: tons of it are sold every Saturday morning at the Kitchener and Waterloo markets. Buy as much as you think you can eat, then double it. It does shrink a little and also it is good to eat cold, especially the smoked kind.

Coil the sausage in your iron frying-pan, cover with boiling water, put a lid on it, and let it boil for about 30 minutes—or longer, or shorter, till the water boils away. If you want, you can then brown it by frying it on top of the stove, pricking the skin to let out the fat or, best of all, put it into your oven at 400°F, or under the broiler to become a perfect, even, rich brown. Serve it with mashed potatoes and a sour cream salad.

Farmers' pork sausage freezes well and makes a quick, easy, emergency meal. It is also great for a loner. Boil the potatoes in their skins along with the sausage.

Jim Morris owns Rundles gourmet restaurant in Stratford, and every day he eats the innovative French and international dishes prepared there. When Jim comes to my house for dinner he says, "Edna, just give me some farmers' pork sausage and lots of potatoes."

LITTLE PORK SAUSAGES

These can be cooked in the same way as the large piece of pork sausage, boiling first in water, then frying, broiling, or browning in a hot oven.

WIENERS AND BUTTONS

Mother considered this a nice, easy dish to make on a busy day.

> 2 or 3 potatoes
> 3 onions
> Batter for egg dumplings (see page 86)
> ¼ to ½ cup butter
> Wieners, as many as you need
> ¼ cup parsley, chopped

Peel and cut the potatoes into inch-thick pieces. Peel and slice the onions. Stir up the egg-dumpling batter and drop bits from a spoon into boiling salted water to cook while the potatoes are boiling, the onions are gently browning in the butter, and the wieners are being heated in boiling water. When all is done, put the buttons (dumplings) in the centre of a platter, arrange the wieners and potatoes nicely round the outside, and pour the onions and browned butter over all of them; then sprinkle on the parsley to make it pretty.

WIENER-KRAUT

Another quickie that Bevvy likes to make.

> ¼ cup butter
> 4 cups green or red cabbage, shredded
> 2 cups apple, chopped
> 5 or 6 wieners, cut in ¼-inch slices
> 2 tablespoons vinegar
> 1½ teaspoons salt
> ½ teaspoon allspice (optional)
> ¼ teaspoon ground cloves (optional)
> ½ cup sour cream

Melt the butter in a frying-pan; add the other ingredients, except the sour cream, and cook over low heat for about 10 minutes until the cabbage is tender but not mushy. Add the sour cream and as soon as it too is heated, the dish is ready to be eaten.

BROTEVASCHT MIT EPPEL (Sausages with Apples)

An old German way that is always welcomed.

    1 or 2 pounds of pork sausage
    6 large cooking apples, peeled and quartered
    2 or 3 tablespoons sugar
    Cinnamon
    ¼ cup currants
    1 wineglass of red wine

Cook the sausages in water for 30 minutes, then in a 400°F oven until nicely browned. Cover the sausages with pieces of apple sprinkled with sugar, cinnamon, and currants. Put a lid on the pan and cook gently in a 350°F oven. When the apples are tender, lift them and the sausages from the pan into a serving dish, pour the wine into the pan, stir it carefully into the juices, boil for a second, then pour over the sausages and apples. Serve with mashed potatoes, a vegetable, and a green salad.

LITTLE SAUSAGES IN BEER

A savoury supper that's quick and easy to make on a night when you lack inspiration.

    18 pork sausages
    1 tablespoon butter
    2 cups onion, thinly sliced
    1½ tablespoons flour
    1 bottle of beer
    1 bay leaf

Brown the sausages in the butter. Remove them from the frying-pan and drain off all but 2 tablespoons of the fat. Sauté the onions in the remaining fat for 10 minutes or until brown. Sprinkle them with flour and stir. Return the sausages to the pan, pour in the beer, and add the bay leaf. Cover and cook over low heat for about 20 minutes.

RUBY'S TOAD IN THE HOLE

To put in 6 individual dishes or one large dish.

> 1 egg
> 1 cup milk
> 1 cup flour
> Salt and pepper
> 6 sausages or more
> 1 or more sliced onions
> 3 tablespoons butter
> ¼ pound mushrooms
> ½ pound tomatoes, sliced

Beat the egg, add the milk, flour, and seasonings. Mix until the batter is smooth and shiny and let stand while you proceed. Put a sausage in each ovenproof dish, or put all in one large dish, and cook in a 400°F oven for 10 minutes while you sauté the onion in butter; add the mushrooms to the onions, then add the tomatoes, and cook for a few minutes. Spread the vegetables over the sausages and sprinkle with salt and pepper. Pour the batter over the vegetables and bake at 400°F for about 30 minutes.

SAUSAGE PUDDING

Like a Yorkshire pudding with sausages as a dividend.

> 1 egg
> 1 cup milk
> 1 cup flour
> Salt and pepper
> 1 pound sausages or wieners

Beat the egg, add the milk, flour and seasonings; let stand while you boil the sausages for about 30 minutes, then brown them in a 400°F oven. Pour the batter over the sausages then return to the oven and bake till the pudding is puffy and brown, about 25 to 30 minutes.

Calvin's Sausingers

Calvin Leaf came to Clara May's house in Neil's Harbour to get a jar of milk.

"I got five cats now I's feedin', but I only wants milk for one, the big he-cat. 'E must'a got in foight, 'e's hurt roight bad, don't go nowhere, just sets all day alongside of I."

"Has he been eating?" I asked.

"Not much, I thought milk moight be good for 'e. I gived 'e cod's tongues, got no bones hinto 'em. 'E loikes 'em, but 'e wouldn't 'ave 'em so I cooked 'em fer meself. Not often I has fish, guess I only 'ad fish four toimes this year; too much trouble to clean it and cook it."

"What do you eat, Calvin?" Clara May asked.

"Oh, I gets pork chops and sausingers, ain't no trouble to 'em, ye just puts in pan and cooks 'em fer a few minutes and they's done." *Calvin stood up to leave us.*

"I hope your cat gets better." I said.

Calvin shook his head. "I near losed 'e one other toime. Couldn't foind 'im fer couple days, I called, 'Kitty, kitty,' and looked all round but nobody'd seed 'im. That evenin' I puts fire in stove to cook me sausingers, just fer nothin' I opened oven door—don't know what maked me do it—and there was cat, 'e jumped roight out, pore t'ing could been roasted."

FOWL

Have you seen how they raise those flabby, little, pale-grey chickens that you buy at the supermarkets? I can't bear to go into one of the long, metal, windowless buildings where, I'm told, thousands of chickens are kept in wire cages hardly large enough for a bird to turn around in, because that might exercise muscles and toughen them, instead of making them tender and fat so they won't take long to cook.

Only occasionally can you go to the farmers' market and find a firm, yellow-skinned hen that's been brought up in a yard, where it could wander all day and eat protein-packed grubs. Those are the chickens you can roast or boil with great expectation of flavour and a rich chicken stock to make soup or milk gravy. Those were the chickens of my childhood.

The modern anemic cage-grown chickens have to get their flavour from whatever you cook with them: honey, orange juice, sour cream, wine, lots of butter, herbs, vegetables, paprika, soya sauce, or mayonnaise, you name it. With plenty of reinforcement they can be very good, too, inexpensive and easy to prepare.

ROAST CHICKEN

In my family this was the most special way to cook a chicken; this was the ultimate, the best meal there was. Mother wouldn't cook chicken any other way for company.

Rinse the bird under the tap, dry it, sprinkle salt in the body cavity, then stuff it—I'll tell you how later. Rub the skin with **soft butter**, sprinkle it with **salt**, then with **flour**. Put the critter on its back in a roasting pan and pop it into a 325°F oven till it's done. I allow plenty of time, 30 minutes per pound, more for a really big capon. If it seems to be browning too fast, I lightly place a crumpled piece of foil over the breast. After the first 30 minutes or so of roasting, I pour half a cupful of water in the bottom of the pan and with it I baste the bird now and then.

The giblets were always a treat in our family: Mother liked the liver, my little sister the heart; Daddy and I took turns with the gizzard. I put them in the pan with the bird, the heart, and liver for just the last hour.

To test if the capon is done, jiggle the drumstick; if it moves readily, the roasting is probably finished; to be doubly sure, insert a sharp, two-pronged fork into the thickest part of the breast or thigh, but not till the leg-moving test has been made and confirmed; you don't want your chick to lose his juices.

When the supreme moment has finally come, lift the bird to a hot platter, make the **brown gravy**, remove the skewers or string used for holding in the dressing, then carry that golden-brown, gorgeous cock to the slavering hoard at your table. You'll never know a prouder moment.

ROAST TURKEY

Every Christmas, newspapers and magazines publish directions for roasting the turkey. I have always followed these directions faithfully and with good results. But this year, when I was having 14 members of my family for Christmas dinner, I decided to cook the bird the way Mother used to do it.

I rinsed the **turkey**, dried it, and sprinkled the cavity with **salt**; then I stuffed it with the same kind of dressing that I use for Roast Chicken (see page 52), except that I doubled the amount and fried a half-pound of cut-up **mushrooms** along with the onions. I rubbed **soft butter** over the skin of the bird, a 16-pounder, sprinkled it lightly with **salt**, and put it on the rack of my large roaster that has a heavy bottom, into which I poured about 2 inches of **water**. I laid the **neck** and **giblets** alongside, covered the pan tightly, and put it on the large burner on top of my stove, where I let it boil and steam gently for 4½ to 5 hours, the same length of time it would have taken to roast the bird. I looked into the pan occasionally during the steaming to be sure the water hadn't disappeared; it hadn't, and I didn't have to add any either.

When the drumsticks were loose and the meat thermometer I'd jabbed into the cavity dressing indicated that the bird was about done, I dribbled soft butter over the skin, sprinkled it with a bit of **white sugar** and **flour**, and put it into a 350°F oven, where it was perfectly browned while the vegetables were cooking on top of the stove.

The drippings in the bottom of the roasting pan were a rich

dark-brown; I removed the fat and made thick, brown gravy.

Everyone in the family agreed it was the best bird they had eaten since Mother used to cook all our Christmas dinners; the meat was deliciously tender and moist. We're going to cook our Christmas turkey the same way next year.

Mother always used to cook her geese, ducks, and chickens that way too.

STUFFING FOR ROAST FOWL

In some of the best dining-rooms, public and private, I've tasted dressings that seemed mouldy or flavoured with soap; I don't like highly seasoned, dark stuffings, that destroy the delicate flavour of the bird; I can't eat dressings that are seasoned with stale, prepared, powdered herbs. The way my mother made her stuffing is the way I try to make mine.

For a 4- or 5-pound bird use

¼ cup butter
1 onion, sliced fine
2 large stalks of celery with leaves, finely chopped
½ a loaf—or a bit more—of not-too-fresh bread, cut
  into cubes or torn into pieces (using the crusts)
3 tablespoons parsley, chopped
Salt and pepper
½ teaspoon dried sage, freshly crushed
2 eggs, slightly beaten
½ cup milk

Melt the butter slowly in a large frying-pan; add the onion and cook slowly till it is soft. Add the celery, and mix it with the onion. Turn off the heat, but keep the pan on the warm burner. Now add the bread; sprinkle over it the parsley, seasonings, and sage; mix thoroughly with the onion, celery, and butter. Beat the eggs and the milk together and pour them over the bread mixture; it should be moistened, but not soggy.

You can make the dressing ahead of time and refrigerate it, but *don't* put it into the bird till you're ready to roast it. Stuff the bird lightly, in the body cavity and around the neck. To keep in the stuffing, truss the body opening with skewers, or sew it with a darning needle and string.

VARIATIONS

WITH MUSHROOMS Sometimes I fry tiny or sliced mushrooms, fresh or canned, and add them to the onions and celery. If I use canned mushrooms, I use the liquid as part of the moistening, instead of all milk.

WITH APPLES Sometimes I add one or two finely sliced apples. If I have non-onion eating guests, I substitute apples for onions.

WITH ROAST TURKEY I sometimes use fewer eggs in the dressing and slightly less liquid. For a very large bird, I double or triple my recipe.

WITH ROAST DUCK AND GOOSE I sometimes use orange or apple juice as my moistener, instead of milk, and I throw in a few raisins.

SAUERKRAUT A goose or a duck stuffed with sauerkraut as dressing is something quite a number of Kitchener-Waterloo old-timers rave about. I've never tried it, but people tell me it's the best.

UNDRESSED BAKED CHICKEN

You can have quite a tasty baked bird without any fuss if you dispense with all the trimmings. Sprinkle the chicken cavity with **garlic salt**. Chuck in a couple of peeled **onions**, and sprigs of **herbs**, **parsley**, and **celery leaves**. Rub **butter** over the skin. Sprinkle on **salt** and **pepper**, dried **herbs**, and **garlic powder**. Put the chicken into a roasting pan, cover, and bake at 325°F until the thighs are almost tender. (Calculate 20 minutes a pound.)

Remove the cover to baste the bird. Increase the heat to 350°F until the chicken is golden brown. It shouldn't take longer than an hour and a half from start to finish, and what a finish!!!

ROAST GOOSE WITH GOOSEBERRY STUFFING

When we locals wanted to celebrate an occasion or give an outsider a treat, we'd go to Kitchener's well-preserved Walper Hotel (built in 1895), where the combination of haute cuisine and German cookery was the most varied and delicious in southwestern Ontario. Joe Zuber, the third of the family owners, gave me this recipe for one of the hotel's favourites.

> **½ pound ground roast veal or roast pork**
> **¼ cup butter**
> **½ cup celery with leaves, diced**
> **1½ cups gooseberries**
> **1-8 ounce package of prepared bread stuffing**
> **3 cups cooked rice**
> **½ cup stock or water**
> **½ teaspoon poultry seasoning**

Brown the ground meat in a pan. Set the meat aside, and melt butter in the pan. Combine the celery, gooseberries, bread stuffing, cooked meat, cooked rice, stock, and seasoning. Mix together lightly with the melted butter.

Stuff and truss the goose, place it, breast up, on a rack in a shallow pan, and roast in a 325°F oven until the leg joints move readily or twist out. An 8-pound goose will take 4 hours to roast; a 10-pound goose will take 4½ hours; a 12-pound goose will take 5 hours, and a 14-pound goose 6 hours. Toward the end of the cooking time, test by moving the drumstick up and down. During the roasting, spoon or siphon off the fat as it gathers in the pan. Save the fat for use in other cooking.

BUTTER-FRIED CHICKEN WITH MILK GRAVY

This is the way Mother cooked chicken most often and the way I like it best, even better than roast chicken, though that was supposed to be the most special. The milk gravy with this could be digested by a 95-year-old grandmother with a stomach ulcer, I'm sure, or a three-month-old baby.

Mother would cut up a nice yellow **hen** into pieces—drumsticks, thighs, wings, back, breast, neck, and giblets; she put the pieces skin-side-up in a kettle, covered them with **boiling**

salted water, and cooked them slowly until they were tender. Then she'd lift out the pieces, drain them, and drop them into melted **butter** in her big iron frying-pan, turning them carefully until all the skin was crisply, delicately browned.

Meanwhile, the **broth** in the kettle would have boiled down to about 3 cupfuls. She'd skim off the pure yellow fat that was floating on top (to be saved for making cookies). Into the broth she'd pour a cup of **milk** (if there was less broth left she'd pour in more milk), bring the mixture almost to a boil, then add a smoothly blended mixture of a ¼ cup of **flour** with another ¾ cup of milk, stirring it as it thickened. Just before serving she'd sprinkle in lots of cut-up fresh **parsley**, at least a ¼ cupful. This gravy, or sauce, poured generously over plain boiled or riced potatoes with the butter-fried chicken and fresh vegetables makes my favourite of all meals, as I think of it at this moment.

And if there's any milk gravy left over, it's wonderful warmed up the next day and poured over buttered bread in a soup plate.

Chicken With Dumplings

If anything could be better than butter-fried chicken with milk gravy, it is butter-fried chicken with dumplings and milk gravy. It is also an easy and wonderful way to stretch a chicken dinner if you find you suddenly have to.

CHICKEN STEW WITH DUMPLINGS

If you'd like a chicken stew, you might add vegetables, carrots, peas, celery, green beans, to the chicken while it's boiling. Cook the dumplings on top, then thicken the broth. The chicken can be served just plain boiled, or fried in butter.

Featherlight Dumplings (page 87)

Featherlight dumplings are foolproof: at a Writers' Union cocktail party, Matt Cohen told me with great enthusiasm that he made them constantly. The first time I invited my mother and father-in-law for dinner, the dumplings spread into a mush on top of the potpie. I guess I was over-anxious. Perhaps I didn't put in enough flour. Maybe I lifted the pot lid too soon. They never failed again.

HINGLE POTPIE (Chicken Potpie)

Both Bevvy and Belle gave me this really old Mennonite recipe; they say it is a special treat for early summer, when the carrots and peas are young and fresh from the garden, but I think it's good any time. They call the noodle squares dumplings.

Cut up a **plump chicken**, or use chicken pieces, and cook till tender with enough salted water to cover well throughout the cooking.

While the chicken is boiling, prepare the noodle-dumplings:

> **2 tablespoons butter**
> **2 cups flour**
> **½ teaspoon of salt**
> **2 eggs, well-beaten**
> **Milk**

Blend the butter with the flour, add the salt and the eggs, and just enough milk to make a very stiff dough. Roll out as thinly as possible on a floured board and let stand for at least 30 minutes. Cut the sheet of dough into 1½-inch squares with a knife.

> **2 potatoes, peeled and sliced ¼-inch thick**
> **12—more or less—tiny new carrots**
> **2 cups fresh peas**
> **Salt and pepper**
> **2 tablespoons parsley, chopped**

When the chicken is tender, put a layer of the potatoes into the bottom of a large kettle, then a layer of the noodle-dumplings, then one of the carrots and peas; sprinkle with salt, pepper, and parsley; put in a layer of chicken, then repeat until all the vegetables and chicken have been put in; the top layer is to be noodles. Pour the boiling chicken broth over all. Cover tightly and don't uncover for 20 minutes while the potpie simmers.

Pour it all into a beautiful bowl and it will be fit for serving a queen, but what queen would ever be lucky enough to get this humble Old Mennonite dish?

EASY WAYS TO COOK CHICKEN

I often spend so much time looking up recipes, that I don't have time to try them. I resort to cooking chicken pieces in one of the following ways, and because it is so quick, so easy, and so good, I wonder why I ever bother with any other. I sprinkle salt and pepper all over the chicken pieces, dip them in flour or crumbs or coat them as I choose, put them skin-side up in a buttered baking pan with a lid, cover for the first 30 minutes in a 350°F oven, have a look, and dab some more coating mixture over each piece, then bake uncovered at 300°F for about 30 minutes longer, till the chicken is tender, golden, and crusty.

BUTTERED CHICKEN

Melt the **butter** and coat the seasoned chicken generously before you bake it.

CHICKEN WITH MAYONNAISE

Coat the chicken with **mayonnaise**. Dip it in fine **breadcrumbs** as well, if you like.

CHICKEN WITH HERBS

Sprinkle **herbs** over coated chicken; it's as simple as that.

SOYA CHICKEN

Beat a ½ cup of **soya sauce** and ¼ cup **cooking oil** together, then dip in the chicken.

HONEY CHICKEN

Drizzle enough **honey**, **brown sugar**, and **soya sauce** to coat the chicken lightly.

CHICKEN WITH ORANGE

Dip the chicken in **butter**, sprinkle with **herbs**, then drizzle the pieces with **orange juice**.

CHICKEN IN CREAM WITH WINE (AND HERBS)

Dredge the chicken pieces in **flour**, spoon over them 1 cup of **sweet or sour cream** diluted with ½ cup of **sherry**. Add **mushrooms** if you like or sprinkle with **herbs** if you can't live without them.

CREAM OF MUSHROOM CHICKEN

Dilute a tin of **mushroom soup** with 1 cup of **cream**, pour it over the chicken, sprinkle it with **paprika**. When it's tender, sprinkle it also with **parsley**, lots of it.

HASTY, TASTY CHICKEN LEGS

Sometimes when Gerry calls, I invite him out for dinner; then I have to think quickly and produce. Because he loves chicken, I often dig out a few legs from my freezer, roll them in some kind of concoction, and put them into my little toaster oven until he comes. We have a drink and the chicken is done. This is a really easy one. The bree (pan juices) can be poured over potatoes boiled in their jackets and sprinkled with parsley, or over potatoes baked with the chicken.

> ¼ **cup sherry**
> ¼ **cup brown sugar**
> **3 tablespoons soya sauce**
> **4 chicken legs**

Stir together the sherry, brown sugar, and soya sauce until the sugar is dissolved. Put the chicken pieces in a baking pan and pour the sauce over them. Bake them at 350°F until tender, about an hour. Turn the pieces over in the sauce occasionally. When the legs are soft and brown, serve them on a heated plate. Pour the sauce over some potatoes or put it in a pitcher to pour over second helpings.

PAPRIKA CHICKEN

I once had a Hungarian friend, who put paprika on everything he cooked; he said it was rich in vitamins and had a bacterial deterrent quality. Anyway, this was very good and easily done on top of the stove.

1 or 2 boilers or chicken pieces, cut up
1 teaspoon of salt
¼ cup butter
2 cups chicken stock or bouillon
1 large onion, sliced fine
2 teaspoons paprika
1 clove garlic, minced
2 green peppers, chopped
¼ cup flour
¼ cup cream
1 cup thick sour cream
2 tablespoons fresh dill or chives, chopped

Lightly sprinkle the chicken pieces with salt and cook slowly in the butter until the meat is golden. Heat the chicken stock. Stir in the onion, paprika, garlic, and green pepper, then add it to the chicken. Cover the pot and let it simmer over low heat for about 40 minutes, or until the chicken is tender, adding more stock if necessary. Remove the chicken from the pot. Place on a heated serving dish and keep hot. Making sure there is at least 1½ cups of stock left in the pot, add blended flour and cream and stir until thickened; lower the heat and stir in the sour cream, being careful not to let the cream boil. Pour the sauce over the chicken; sprinkle with dill or chives. Serve with buttered noodles or rice and a green salad.

SWEET AND SOUR CHICKEN

This is a top-of-the-stove way to make chicken taste good.

> **1 chicken, cut into serving pieces**
> **2 tablespoons cooking oil**
> **2 tablespoons butter**
> **1 clove of garlic, minced**
> **1 teaspoon salt**
> **Sprinkle of pepper**
> **3 tablespoons lemon juice**
> **½ cup tomato sauce (or 3 tomatoes)**
> **1 cup chicken broth, or beer, or wine**
> **2 tablespoons molasses**
> **¼ cup raisins (optional)**
> **¼ cup sliced, buttered almonds or shelled**
>   **sunflower seeds**

Brown the chicken pieces all round in the oil and butter. Blend the minced garlic, salt and pepper, lemon juice, tomato sauce, broth, and molasses. Pour into the pan with the chicken. Cover and simmer for about 45 minutes or until the chicken is tender. Add the raisins and simmer a few minutes longer. Sprinkle with almonds just before serving with noodles or rice.

SESAME SOYA CHICKEN

This is another easy-to-prepare chicken dish. You can let it bake while you play a game or two of Parcheesi.

> **¼ cup butter**
> **¼ cup honey**
> **1 tablespoon lemon juice**
> **1 tablespoon soya sauce**
> **Chicken pieces for 3 or 4 eaters**
> **Sesame seeds**

In a flat baking dish, melt the butter; blend in the honey, lemon juice, and soya sauce. Dip the chicken pieces in the mixture to moisten all over, then sprinkle liberally with sesame seeds. Place the chicken pieces skin-side up in the pan. Bake uncovered at 350°F for about 1 hour, or until tender, basting occasionally with the soya mixture. You might need to add ½ cup of water to keep the sauce from burning. Put some potatoes and carrots into the oven at the same time, so you can eat as soon as the Parcheesi game is over.

CRISP OVEN-FRIED CHICKEN

This is so easy and so good; one of my absolute favourites. You can make it for one, two, or twenty.

> ½ **cup butter**
> 1 **clove garlic, crushed, or minced, or juiced**
> 1 **cup dry breadcrumbs**
> ½ **cup grated cheese**
> ¼ **cup shelled sunflower seeds, or chopped**
>   **almonds, or sesame seeds**
> 3 **tablespoons parsley, chopped**
> 1 **teaspoon of salt**
> **Pepper**
> ½ **teaspoon of thyme or summer savoury**
> 1 **small chicken or pieces of chicken, cut up; I**
> **prefer breasts cut in half, or drumsticks and thighs**

In a 13" x 9" x 2" cake pan, melt the butter with the garlic while your oven is heating to 350°F. Mix all the other ingredients, except the chicken, in a shallow dish. First dip the chicken pieces into the melted butter, then coat with the crumb mixture. Place them skin-side up in the pan—not overlapping. If you have any crumbs left over, spread them over the chicken. Bake at 350°F for about an hour, or until tender. Baste a couple of times with pan drippings till crisp and brown. Serve from the pan at the table. Baked potatoes and baked squash or any vegetables go well with this super dish.

NORM'S SWISS CHICKEN CUTLETS

When Norm is planning a dinner party for 12, she can prepare these the day before, keep them in a cool place, and simply have to put them in the oven when the first guests arrive. After a drink or two, the guests can hardly wait to get at them. They are delicious, and tender enough to be eaten with only a fork.

> **12 large chicken breasts, boned and skinned**
> ½ **teaspoon of salt**
> ⅛ **teaspoon of pepper**
> **2 eggs, beaten**
> **1 cup fine breadcrumbs**
> **3 tablespoons vegetable oil**
> **3 tablespoons butter**
> ½ **cup flour**
> **Salt and pepper**
> 2½ **cups milk**
> ½ **cup dry white wine**
> **1 cup grated cheese**

Cut each breast into 4 pieces. Sprinkle the pieces with salt and pepper. Dip them in beaten eggs, then in the breadcrumbs. Heat the oil in a large pan and brown the cutlets for 3 minutes on each side. To make the sauce, in a saucepan over medium heat, melt the butter. Add the flour, with salt and pepper to taste. Add milk all at once, stirring, until the sauce thickens. Remove from heat and add the wine. Pour half of the sauce into a large baking pan, put in the cutlets, then pour the rest of the sauce all over them. Cover and chill overnight. Bake, covered, at 350°F for 50 minutes, or until the chicken is tender. Sprinkle with cheese, then return to the oven for 2 more minutes.

BRUSSELS OR BROCCOLI DIVAN

This is a great company dish.

Chicken or turkey pieces
1 quart Brussels sprouts or broccoli

Sauce:

¼ **cup butter**
3 tablespoons flour
½ **teaspoon curry powder (optional)**
2 cups hot broth or milk
1 cup Cheddar cheese, grated
1 cup sour cream
3 tablespoons dry sherry or white wine
1 teaspoon Worcestershire sauce

Simmer the chicken or turkey pieces in salted water until tender. Cook the sprouts or broccoli in salted water until just tender, then drain. Make the sauce: melt the butter, blend in the flour and curry; vigorously stir in the hot broth or milk, stirring until the sauce is thickened and smooth. Bone the cooked meat. Arrange the vegetables on a deep, heat-proof serving platter or flat-bottomed casserole, sprinkle them lightly with half of the cheese, arrange the chicken slices over the top. Combine the sour cream with the sauce, stir in the sherry and Worcestershire sauce, pour it over the chicken. Sprinkle with the remaining cheese. Place about 5 inches below high heat, in a preheated broiler until browned and bubbly, or put in a 300°F oven till your guests have finished their apéritifs.

Norm's Soya Rice (page 89) and squash, baked and whipped with butter and cream, make this a memorable meal.

POULET ENDORMI (Chicken on a Bed of Rice)

I made this one day when Pierre and Janet were coming for dinner; the next night I had it again with Lorna and Ross; the night after that, with Pam and Gerry. You can't trust rice, it never knows when to stop.

**As many chicken pieces as you think you need
(I added some after my second dinner)
1½ teaspoons of salt
½ teaspoon of pepper
Sprinkle of paprika
2 tablespoons cooking oil
2 tablespoons butter
1 cup onion, sliced
1 clove garlic, minced
2 to 4 cups chicken broth or bouillon
1 cup white wine (in place of as much broth)
3 to 4 cups tomatoes, canned, frozen, or fresh
1 cup celery, sliced
1 cup carrots, sliced
1 cup peas
1 cup rice, uncooked
1 bay leaf
½ teaspoon thyme
½ teaspoon tarragon
½ teaspoon oregano
½ cup parsley, chopped**

Season the chicken with salt, pepper and paprika. Heat the oil and butter in a frying-pan and brown the pieces of chicken on all sides. Remove and keep warm. In the same pan put the onion and garlic, sauté until the onion is tender. Add 2 cups of the chicken broth and the wine, and stir to loosen all the brown bits in the pan. Put in the tomatoes, and bring to a boil, then stir in all the rest of the ingredients, except the parsley, which should be added just before serving. Scrape all into a baking dish, put the chicken on top, cover tightly, put the dish in a 325°F oven and forget about it for almost an hour, though it might be wise to look in at half time to add more chicken broth, rice being the greedy thing that it is. The dish will be fuller than it was when you started. It's great to have enough for three meals, or enough for nine people at one. Don't underestimate the chicken.

With this I served Pierre's favourite Schnippled Bean Salad.

CHICKEN VELVET

This is a super smooth way to serve all your nutrients in one dish. You can prepare it in advance and have it simmering gently to tantalize your guests as they arrive.

2 tablespoons cooking oil
2 tablespoons butter
3 or 4 pounds of chicken pieces

Heat the oil and butter in a large frying-pan and sauté the pieces of chicken over medium heat until browned on all sides. Meanwhile, in your blender put:

2 medium tomatoes, quartered, or 1 cup canned
1 onion, quartered
1 carrot, coarsely diced
1 stalk of celery, chopped
1 clove garlic (optional)
1½ teaspoons salt
¼ teaspoon pepper

Blend for a few seconds then add:

6 sprigs of parsley
¼ cup dry sherry, white wine, or lemon juice
½ teaspoon rosemary
¼ teaspoon tarragon (optional)

Cover and blend on high speed for 30 seconds. Pour over the browned chicken in the frying-pan, cover and simmer for 45 minutes or until the chicken is tender, stirring occasionally. Add: 1 cup mushrooms, sliced (optional), half an hour before serving time. Pour all into a large, hot serving dish and be prepared to ladle the chicken and that lovely sauce over cooked rice, potatoes, or noodles. Serve with a green salad.

RUNDLES POULET SAUTÉ CHASSEUR
(Huntsmen's Chicken)

The *chef de cuisine*, John Walker, said this is a good way to put some flavour into those watery, limp pieces of chicken that have never seen the light of day.

¼ cup butter
Salt and pepper
1 frying chicken, or pieces
¼ cup shallots or green onions, chopped
1 cup sliced or button mushrooms
½ cup dry white wine
1 cup demi glace or chicken broth
1 cup fresh tomatoes, peeled and chopped
Parsley and tarragon, chopped

Melt the butter in a pan over a fairly hot fire. Season the pieces of chicken and place them in the pan. Cook to a golden brown on all sides, cover with a lid, and cook for a few more minutes. Lift the pieces with tongs into an entrée dish that can be put in the oven. Drop the shallots into the pan, cover, and cook for a few minutes without browning them; add the mushrooms, cover, and cook gently for 3 to 4 minutes. Drain off the fat, add the wine and demi glace if you have any, or chicken broth, or bouillon. Add the tomatoes and simmer for 5 minutes. Correct the seasoning, pour the whole bit over the chicken in the entrée dish, and put it into a 300°F oven until the chicken is tender or till you're ready to serve it. Sprinkle it then, with parsley and tarragon.

Sorry about not giving you the demi glace recipe: John makes the French sauces so easily—by adding certain ingredients to other sauces he comes up with a new one. A demi glace is a derivative of sauce espagnole. (You'll have to go to Rundles to get a real Poulet Sauté Chasseur.) The day of our eighth lesson, in his Stylish Entertainment course, John made and served us Lobster Soufflé Suidoise, Poulet Chasseur with a green salad, Irish soda bread, and for dessert Gateaux Mille Fuille. The meal was a triumph. The French really care enough about food to spend time preparing it. Whenever it's served to me, I make great resolutions, but at home my laziness overcomes me and I'm happy with potpie.

Freezing Fowl

Wrap individual servings of fowl in foil, put all the wrapped pieces in a freezer bag. Don't let them get lost by themselves in the freezer or you won't find them till your annual clean out.

Chicken Bones

The day after I cook a chicken or a number of chicken pieces, I put the bones into a pot, cover them with water, and simmer them for an hour or so. I then strain the bones, cool the broth, and put it into my fridge, where it jells and I can later use it for soup or a casserole.

I put the bones in a plastic bag in a well-protected garbage container, instead of into my compost, where little animals or dogs might find them.

David and Bevvy Martin had a beautiful border collie whom they dearly loved and cared for. One day Lassie found chicken bones in somebody's compost. She became very sick and had to be put down because the brittle, sharp bones had pierced her vital innards and she couldn't be saved.

FISH AND SHELLFISH

Until I started living in my cottage on Sunfish Lake, I was sorry that my pioneering ancestors had settled in a completely land-locked county that had only little lakes and rivers. I longed for ships and great seas. My father was brought up on part of his great-grandfather's land, which ran for two miles along the Conestoga River, where as a boy little Johnny went fishing every chance he got.

When we were very young, Daddy used to take us fishing along the Conestoga's low, safe banks. If we were exceptionally lucky, we caught enough chubs and shiners to give everyone in the family a taste. Daddy cleaned the tiny fishes; Mother dipped them in flour or in egg and breadcrumbs, and fried them in butter till they were crisp and golden. No fish has ever tasted so good, not even the brook trout, black-bass, and lake trout that Daddy caught and brought home from fishing trips in faraway places with "The Men."

Bevvy and David live on the land along the Conestoga where her great-great-grandparents settled and, while I visited them for a week in the spring, Salome, Lyddy and Amsey went fishing, and Bevvy fried the chubs and shiners in the same way that Mother used to fry them for us.

Mother never cooked fish any other way, except tinned salmon and smoked finnan haddie.

Codfish

I remember when people used to spurn codfish as an inferior, coarse kind of fish that they'd eat only if they were starving. Since the price of cod has gone up, it has become more respectable and there are many fine ways of preparing it.

Of course, the best way is done in Neil's Harbour where Henry would catch it, split it, and carry it home from the shore by the tail and within 15 minutes of its demise in the sea, Clara Mae would cook it in butter.

COD CRISP

Here is my favourite inland method: Lay slices of **cod** in a well-buttered baking dish, **salt** it lightly, and spread with a **bread dressing** made with cubes of soft **bread** or fine, soft crumbs, **onion minced, melted butter, summer savory**, and enough **milk** to moisten it when it's all mixed together. Now cover the dressing generously with finely cut-up **bacon**, fat and lean. Bake it in a 450°F oven for about 10 minutes; by then the fish should be done and the bacon crisp. Serve it with mashed potatoes and vegetables or just with a crisp green salad.

Fishermen's Meals

Because Tom Candle's stage in Neil's Harbour is placed on a slight crook in the row of stages, its doorway commands a long view of the road from the Cabot Trail in Cape Breton. As he mended his nets and talked, Tom kept watching everything that moved.

Tom: "Look, look at the crowd in that car. Pity somebody ain't here with a restaurant. 'E'd make a pile o' money."

A fisherman sitting on a chair in the doorway: "Too hard to git meat fer it; meat's been some scarce this summer. I'd fancy a bit o' meat one o' these days, ain't tasted nothin' but fish for near three weeks."

Me: "What else do you have?"

Tom: "It wouldn't seem like Saturday if we didn't have baked beans for supper. Sundays we has boiled taties, cabbage, salt or fresh meat, and puddin'; always beans for breakfast."

Chair: "Sometimes we has heggs 'n' jam-bread, 'n' cornmeal porridge; some mornings it's dried fish and taties with pork fat fried out and onions boiled together; we soak the fish night before and us men gets it ready ourself."

Tom: "Fer supper we 'ave fish or fish cakes made o' leftovers or hash made from boiled dinners, or pancakes. We eats good. Trouble wif people nowdays is they eats too light food."

Chair: "Tom, you goin' shave fer bean feed in Hall tonight?"

Tom: "No, I only shaves on Saturday. Too hot fer bean feed but I'll go and chase the women." He grinned wickedly at me. "You want to look out fer me, I'm a terrible, terrible man."

FRIED OR GRILLED FILLETS

Overcooked fish is dry and tough; cover the fillets for the few minutes it takes to cook them.

Cut the **fish** into serving portions, sprinkle them with **salt** and **lemon juice**, and let stand for 10 to 15 minutes. Dip each piece in **milk**, then **flour**, or **bread crumbs**. Fry the pieces in a lightly-buttered skillet for only a few minutes on each side, depending on the thickness of the fillet. The moment the raw look or feel is gone, garnish with parsley or lemon slices and you'll have a delicacy.

To grill the fillets prepare the same way, but put the pieces in a buttered pan, dot them with butter, and put under a grill, turning only once when slightly browned on top.

BAKED FILLETS WITH LEMON BUTTER

I think this is my favourite way to serve fish. Simple, easy, and foolproof, if you keep your eye on it. My sister Norm says she doesn't like fish, but she liked this, and her husband, Ralph, had three servings.

> **2 pounds fish fillets**
> **2 tablespoons parsley, finely chopped**
> **¼ cup butter, melted**
> **2 tablespoons lemon juice**
> **½ teaspoon of salt**
> **Pepper**

Cut the fillets into serving pieces and fit them into a buttered baking dish so they don't overlap. Sprinkle generously with the parsley, or any herb you prefer. Combine the remaining ingredients. Pour over the fillets. Bake at 450°F until the fish is opaque and flakes readily when pierced by a fork; don't overbake. Serve immediately, spooning hot sauce over the fish.

BAKED FISH STEAKS OR FILLETS

Frozen fish steaks or fillets are the loner's dream; it is so easy to thaw them and have a nourishing meal. Great for emergency cooking as well.

2 pounds fish steaks or fillets
Juice of 1 lemon
2 tablespoons butter
2 tablespoons flour
½ teaspoon of salt
Pepper
½ teaspoon of paprika
1 small can of mushrooms with liquid
Milk
½ cup of grated Cheddar cheese

Place the fish steaks in a buttered baking pan; squeeze the lemon juice over them. Melt the butter and stir in the flour and seasonings, then the liquid drained from the mushrooms, plus enough milk to make 1 cup; stir slowly into the flour mixture until thickened. Pour the sauce over the fish. Sprinkle with mushrooms and cheese. Bake at 350°F for 30 minutes or less, until the fish is just baked.

FINNAN HADDIE

I don't know why finnan haddie is supposed to be humble; I think it's a treat.

Buy a thick, fresh-looking, golden piece of **fish** and simmer it in water until it is just tender. Make a medium-thick **cream sauce** (page 80), (lots of it), add to it cut up gobs of **parsley** and as many hot, **hard-boiled eggs** as you like. Now you can pour the sauce over the whole piece of fish, or flake the fish into the sauce as I do. Serve it with mild vegetables, a salad, or on buttered toast, or with hot biscuits or buns.

WHOLE SALMON COOKED IN COURT BOUILLON

The best salmon I have ever tasted, was made by John Walker during our Stylish Entertainment course at Rundles Restaurant in Stratford. A great dish for a supper party or a large family.

Court bouillon can be used to cook lobster and other fish, as well as salmon.

1 quart water
½ cup carrots, sliced
½ cup onion, sliced
¼ cup vinegar or white wine
2 or 3 parsley stalks
6 peppercorns
1 bay leaf
2 ½ teaspoons salt
Sprig of thyme

Simmer all the ingredients for 30 to 40 minutes, then strain.

Meanwhile, prepare a firm, fresh, odourless salmon: remove all the scales with the back of a knife so you won't cut the skin. Remove the gills, intestines, and blood from the backbone. Clean out the head, or remove it if the glazed eyes upset you.

Wrap the fish in a long piece of foil with the ends twisted like handles to lift the fish out of the bouillon after it's cooked. Seal the foil across the top and prick holes throughout its length to let the bouillon flavour the fish. In a pot long enough to hold the salmon without bending it, place the foiled fish in the strained bouillon. The liquid should cover the fish. Bring it slowly to a boil; skim, then simmer very slowly with a lid on so the steam stays in: 15 minutes for a 7-pound fish, 20 minutes for 14 pounds.

Unwrap, cut into the center bone in the thickest part. If it's done, it will flake away. Salmon must be served at once; you can't reheat it and expect it to be as good, but you could rewrap it in foil with herb butter inside its cavity and keep it warm in a low oven for a very little while; or serve it cold, letting it cool to room temperature and then skinning it.

Keen on presentation, John placed the salmon on a platter surrounded with little mounds of various *al dente* vegetables, sprigs of parsley, dill, and twists of sliced lemon as a garnish, on the fish. Several people in the class took its picture.

John said, "Don't spoil it with bits of this and that. The fashion today is to keep it simple, never elaborate."

At the table, the fish was served with Aioli Sauce (page 82) in a sauce boat, and mayonnaise for those who didn't like garlic.

SALMON LOAF

Mother usually baked potatoes when she made this loaf, and served it with a sour cream salad.

1 ½ cups milk
¾ cup breadcrumbs
3 eggs, separated
2 cups flaked salmon
Salt and pepper
2 tablespoons lemon juice
Rind of ½ lemon
1 stalk celery, cut up (optional)

Scald the milk, add the breadcrumbs; cook for 5 minutes, stirring constantly over boiling water in a double boiler; add 3 beaten egg yolks and cook 5 minutes longer, stirring. Cool slightly. Add salmon, salt and pepper, lemon juice, and rind. Fold in 3 egg whites, stiffly beaten, then turn everything into a greased loaf pan. Set the dish in a pan of hot water and bake for 45 minutes at 350°F.

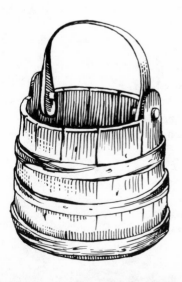

SALMON PATTIES

When she wanted a quick meal, Mother often made these; we liked them with mashed potatoes and a lettuce salad.

1 tin of salmon
2 eggs, beaten slightly
Pepper
1 stalk celery (optional)
Parsley, chopped
Breadcrumbs

Mother removed the skin and bones from the salmon. (I don't, I squash them with a fork and mash them in the rest; they probably do you some good.) Then she put in the eggs, pepper, celery, parsley, and just enough crumbs to make the mixture dry enough to make patties. Dropping tablespoonfuls of salmon into a dish of breadcrumbs, she would roll them around, shape them into patties, and fry them slowly in butter till they were golden brown and firm. I like mine with Lemon Butter Sauce. (Page 81)

BAKED SCALLOPS

Quite a long time ago, when I was waiting at Digby Harbour, Nova Scotia, for the ferry to take me across the Bay of Fundy I watched the fishermen unloading the scallops they had just dredged up from the bottom of the sea. I bought two dozen scallop shells, perfect for serving Coquille St. Jacques at a ladies' luncheon.

1 pound scallops
Salt and pepper
2 tablespoons butter
½ cup onion, sliced
1 ½ cups celery, chopped
1 cup mushrooms, sliced

Cream Sauce:
¼ cup butter
¼ cup flour
½ teaspoon salt
2 cups hot milk

Topping:
⅓ cup butter
1 cup breadcrumbs
¼ cup cheese, finely grated

Sprinkle the scallops with salt and pepper. In the 2 tablespoons of butter, sauté the onion, celery, and mushrooms until limp. Make a medium-thick cream sauce by melting the ¼ cup butter, adding the flour, salt, and hot milk, and stirring until thickened. Add the scallops and partially-cooked vegetables. Pour into a buttered casserole. Top with buttered breadcrumbs and grated cheese. Bake at 375°F about 20 to 30 minutes, until the crumbs are nicely browned and the scallop mixture is bubbly.

COQUILLE ST. JACQUES

If you have scallop shells, this is impressive. Follow the baked scallop recipe, but instead of pouring the mixture into a casserole, spoon it into scallop shells and put a rim of mashed potatoes around the edge of each shell to keep the scallops from running over, when you put them into the oven, sprinkled with buttered crumbs. Bake at 350°F for about 25 minutes. Serve the hot shells on a plate with a salad and the ladies will think they are eating at the Ritz in Paris.

FRIED SCALLOPS

Fried Scallops are one of my favourite foods. Because they are so delicate, I prefer my scallops pure.

1 pound scallops
Salt
Flour
1 egg, beaten
¾ cup fine breadcrumbs
¼ cup of butter
Lemon wedges

Sprinkle the scallops with salt. Roll each one in flour; dip in the beaten egg, then roll in the breadcrumbs. Fry in butter until golden all over. Serve with lemon wedges.

HOT SUSSEX SMOKIES

This was the first course of a dinner Joan and John Coward served in their home on the edge of the Sussex Downs. The smokies were served in individual ramekins and followed by chicken pie, salad, a bowl of fruit, apricot mousse, and cheese with biscuits. Then we sat in their charming living-room and watched the sheep strolling on the Downs at the end of their garden. Quite frankly, I could have eaten more smokies, (smoked mackerel), if there'd been more. Instead of individual ramekins, I think they could be prepared in a baking dish, that might have allowed second helpings, and perhaps made with other smoked fish.

> **4 small smokies (smoked mackerel)**
> **1 cup cream (the richer the better)**
> **4 small tomatoes, fresh or canned**
> **Pepper**
> **1 cup cheese, grated (Joan used Gruyère, but you**
>   **could use another mild cheese)**

Remove all of the bones and flake the fish. Put ½ cup of the cream into a shallow, buttered earthenware dish or into individual ramekins. Add the flaked fish.

Remove the seeds from the tomatoes, chop roughly, and spread over the fish. Sprinkle with pepper; pour on the remaining ½ cup of cream. Sprinkle with cheese and bake at 350°F for 20 minutes. Glaze for about 3 minutes under a very hot grill.

FRIED OYSTERS

Several times during the week, I stayed with Gordon and Ivy Wagner in their lovely home on Comox Bay, British Columbia, where Gordon wrote his first book, *From My Window*. Gordon fried fresh oysters for our lunch. When I came home, I discovered that I had gained 10 pounds, but those fried oysters were worth it.

Gordon dipped each **oyster** in lightly beaten **eggs**, then coated each in fine **breadcrumbs**. In a frying-pan, he melted lots of **butter**, put in the oysters, and sprinkled them with **salt**

and pepper. He hovered over them for about five minutes. When they were golden on the bottom, he turned them over to brown on the other side. With lemon wedges and a salad, we didn't want anything more.

SCALLOPED OYSTERS

When Gordon Wagner comes to Ontario to promote a new book, he brings me the fattest, fresh oysters I have ever seen. He fries a batch for our lunch, and I freeze the rest in plastic containers of various sizes, so I can use them in an oyster stew or fry a few for lunch. The largest containers (1 pint) I save until Pamela Berton comes in the winter, and we eat the whole lot in one glorious binge.

> **1 pint of oysters**
> **⅓ cup of butter**
> **2 cups fine breadcrumbs (I use herbed bread**
> **stuffing that comes in a box and give it a whirl**
> **in my food processor)**
> **½ teaspoon salt**
> **⅓ cup Parmesan, grated**
> **Liquid from drained oysters**
> **½ cup of white wine or sherry**

I thaw the oysters until I can separate them. Then I drain them and save the liquid. Melt the butter in a shallow baking pan, 8" x 8" or 6" x 10". Stir in the breadcrumbs, salt, and Parmesan. Take out about half of the crumbs and level those left in the pan; place the oysters over them. Blend the oyster liquid and wine and pour it over the oysters. Sprinkle on the remaining crumbs and bake, uncovered, at 375°F for 25 minutes until lightly browned. When the oysters are served with a salad and a good wine, Pamela and I eat every crumb.

MEAT AND FISH ACCOMPANIMENTS

*Besides relishes, ketchup, pickles, celery, cauliflower,
and carrot sticks, Mother always had other special
accompaniments for different meats on her table at dinner:
cranberries with turkey and chicken, spiced gooseberries
with goose, raisin sauce with ham or beef tongue, apple
halves with chicken and pork, hot or cold horseradish
sauce with beef, and sliced Spanish onions in vinegar with
sausages.*

PARSLEY SAUCE

As you can see, this is just an ordinary cream sauce with parsley
added. You could add a number of other things instead, like
cheese, herbs, or whatever you fancy. It is great with salmon,
but would make any fish taste good.

　　1 tablespoon of butter
　　1 tablespoon of flour
　　½ teaspoon of salt
　　Pepper
　　1 cup milk
　　3 tablespoons parsley, chopped

Melt the butter in a saucepan over low heat. Blend in the flour,
salt, and pepper. Add the milk gradually and cook, stirring,
until the sauce thickens. Remove from heat and add parsley.

WHITE CREAM SAUCE

　　2 tablespoons butter
　　2 tablespoons flour
　　1 cup milk
　　Salt and pepper

Melt the butter. Blend in the flour. Slowly stir in the milk until
the sauce thickens.

LEMON BUTTER SAUCE

Wonderful with any fish, bland or strong. Put it into a sauce dish on the table and help yourself; I always pour it all over my fish, others seem to like little dabs.

¼ **cup butter**
1 ½ **tablespoons flour**
1 **tablespoon sugar**
½ **cup water**
Juice of 1 large lemon

Melt the butter, stir in the flour and sugar, then the water and lemon; stir till it thickens. Taste it, if it seems too sour, add a bit more sugar.

PARSLEY BUTTER

Great with grilled steak, fish, asparagus, broccoli, or anything that requires little cooking.

½ **cup butter**
Juice of ¼ lemon
¼ **to ½ teaspoon parsley, finely chopped**
Salt and pepper

Combine all the ingredients with softened butter and blend well. Shape into a roll one inch in diameter. Place in wet greaseproof paper and let it harden in the fridge, or keep it frozen till you want it. Put about a ¼-inch slice on top of each serving of sizzling-hot meat.

HERB BUTTER

Very nice with lamb, zucchini, and so forth. Made the same way as Parsley Butter, but using a blend of **thyme,** **oregano,** *and* **basil.** *You could vary the herbs, but don't use sage on lamb, save it for pork or goose.*

GARLIC BUTTER

Great on steak or to make garlic bread. Crush a clove or two of **garlic** till it becomes very soft, before blending with the butter.

OTHER BUTTERS

To the butter, lemon juice, salt and pepper, add very finely chopped green peppers, or black olives, or anchovies, or caviar, or mushrooms, to give different flavours to various foods. You must use them discreetly.

Jeanne's Sauce For Fish

Almost every morning in Brittany, Françoise would drive Jeanne and me to the nearby village of Tregunc, where a van was parked in the square. One side was open to display innumerable kinds of fish and shellfish caught earlier that morning in the sea.

Françoise and Jeanne would make their selection, and as an appetizer for dinner there might be a platter of langustine, which Françoise adeptly opened for me. Or there would be a whole fish baked or grilled and served with a rich yellow sauce from a silver sauce boat.

"Jeanne is very good with fish," Françoise told me. "If you wish, you may watch how she makes the sauce."

*In her beloved kitchen, Jeanne had peeled and sliced three or four **shallots** and gently simmered them in half a cupful of **wine vinegar**. She strained out the shallots, poured the flavoured vinegar into a bowl, which she held over a pot of hot but not boiling water. She put about a teaspoon of **butter** into the vinegar and stirred it with a well-worn wooden spoon. Then she added another spoonful of butter and beat it in. Then another and another, stirring and beating well every time until she had added half a pound of the butter! The sauce was homogenized, rich yellow and would make any old fish taste wonderful.*

Horse-Radish

I don't know whether bottled horse-radish wasn't sold in the olden days when I was young, or whether my parents were masochistic. Anyway, Mother bought the fresh, tough, knobbly roots at the market and peeled them, with tears streaming down her face, while Daddy, also streaming, put them through the food chopper. Mother added vinegar and sugar to taste; they almost gasped as they ate it. I wouldn't even taste horse-radish; I figured anything that made Mother and Daddy cry was up to no good.

HOT HORSE-RADISH SAUCE

They loved this with roast or boiled beef.

1 cup milk
1 egg
2 tablespoons butter
2 tablespoons of flour
1 tablespoon of white sugar
Pinch of salt
2 tablespoons grated horse-radish

Mix all but the horse-radish and stir over medium heat until thick, then add the horse-radish. Serve hot, hot, hot.

HORSE-RADISH JELL-O

Ruby says this goes over big.
   Dissolve 1 small (3 ¼ oz.) package of **lemon Jell-O** in 1 ½ cups boiling water. Chill until it is about to set, then fold in:

½ cup of mayonnaise
4 tablespoons prepared horse-radish
¼ teaspoon of salt
½ cup heavy cream, whipped

If you like, you might add 5 tablespoons of sliced, stuffed olives and ½ teaspoon of paprika. Chill until set.

AIOLI SAUCE (Garlic Sauce)

This richly flavoured, smooth sauce is delicious with fish or beef. It is very popular in France, and at Rundles Restaurant in Stratford.

> **4 fat cloves garlic per person**
> **⅛ teaspoon salt**
> **2 egg yolks**
> **1 cup olive oil**
> **Freshly ground black pepper**
> **1 teaspoon lemon juice**

Crush the garlic to a smooth paste in a mortar with salt; blend in the egg yolks until the mixture is smooth and homogenous. Add the olive oil drop by drop at first, then in a thin trickle, whisking the mixture till your arm feels it. The Aioli will thicken gradually until it makes a stiff, firm consistency. Season to taste with additional salt, a little pepper, and the lemon juice; serve chilled in a sauce boat.

NORM'S NIPPY MUSTARD

Some people like this with ham, some with beef.

> **½ cup dry mustard**
> **½ cup brown sugar**
> **¼ cup vegetable oil**
> **¼ cup horse-radish**
> **¼ cup cider vinegar**

Mix together the dry mustard and sugar. Stir in the oil, horseradish and vinegar until it is smoothly blended. Spoon into small jars, and cover tightly. It will keep for months.

CRANBERRY SAUCE

We always have this with turkey or roast chicken.

4 cups of cranberries
2 cups of sugar
2 cups of water

Boil all together without stirring, until all the skins of the cranberries pop (about 5 minutes). Cool and serve. It will keep for ages in your fridge.

SPICED GOOSEBERRIES

Guess what? It's great with roast goose or any bird, or pork.

1 cup of vinegar
3 cups of brown sugar
6 cups gooseberries
1 tablespoon of cinnamon
1 teaspoon of ground cloves

Bring the vinegar and brown sugar to a boil, then put in the berries and spices. Cook for about 20 minutes and serve hot or cold. This sauce can also be kept in sterilized jars.

RAISIN SAUCE

Try it with cold meats, or hot with hot tongue.

2 tablespoons of butter
2 tablespoons of flour
1 ½ cups cider or fruit juice, or water, or broth
½ cup of raisins

Blend the butter and flour, add the juice and raisins, and cook until the mixture boils, stirring constantly. Simmer for about 10 minutes until thickened. Serve hot with ham. Sometimes I'll add a bit of sherry; if my ham hasn't a fancy glaze, I'll also put in ¾ of a teaspoon of mustard.

NORM'S APPLE HALVES

Norm prefers to use Northern Spies, but any firm cooking apples will do. She peels the **apples**, cuts them in half, removes the core, and places the apples flat-side down in a flat-bottomed cooking pot. She pours in about ¼ to ½ a cup of water and turns on the heat, watching the apples while they cook, turning them when they are soft on the bottom, but making sure they do not cook too fast or too long, and lose their firmness and shape. She then sprinkles them with white **sugar** and a bit of **cinnamon**, carefully lifts them, one at a time, onto a flat serving dish to be eaten hot or cold with chicken or fresh pork. This is much better than apple sauce.

STUFFED APPLES

Easy and simple to bake along with a roast of pork or spareribs.

1 onion
Drippings or butter
2 crumbled sage leaves
¼ cup raisins, soaked and chopped
Salt and pepper
1 cup of breadcrumbs
6 apples

Chop the onion and cook it in some drippings from the roast (or in butter), add sage, raisins, salt, pepper, and breadcrumbs and 2 or 3 more tablespoons of drippings; brown all slightly. Core the apples and stuff them with the mixture. Put the apples around the roast about three-quarters of an hour before the meat is ready to come out. Without a lid, keep roasting at 350°F till the apples are soft, but not mushy. These are good with sausages, too.

FEATHERLIGHT DUMPLINGS

White, fluffy dumplings, supposed to be foolproof.

2 cups of flour
4 teaspoons baking powder
½ teaspoon of salt
Milk

Sift the dry ingredients and add only enough milk to make a stiff dough—not at all runny. Drop tablespoonsful of thick batter into the boiling broth, cover tightly, cook gently, and don't lift the lid for 10 minutes. Then lift the lid and sigh with relief. The dumplings will be snowy white puffs.

OIYA KNEPP (Egg Dumplings)

These dumplings are slightly heavier than Featherlight Dumplings, but have more flavour.

2 cups of flour
1 teaspoon of salt
4 teaspoons of baking powder
¼ teaspoon of pepper
3 tablespoons of melted shortening
1 egg, well beaten
Milk

Sift the dry ingredients, add melted shortening, egg, and just enough milk to make a moist, stiff batter that you can plop by tablespoonsful into boiling liquid; reduce the heat and cook gently, with the dumplings tightly covered, for 15 minutes. Don't peek or your dumplings will be tough and heavy, though sometimes I rather like them that way.

Buttered Noodles

*Quite often, when I go to Bevvy's for supper, she has a bowl
of hot noodles with butter melted over them to be eaten
with summer sausage and all the other things, like pickled
beets, and cheese, relish, celery, and salad. Sometimes,
Bevvy stirs a cupful of cooked peas into the noodles.*

*Mother often used to melt butter in a frying-pan, pour in
the noodles, and stir them around with lots of cut up
parsley. Sometimes, she'd scatter brown, buttered crumbs
over them when she served them. Sometimes, she left them
in the frying-pan until they were brown on the bottom;
she'd flip them over and brown the other side as well. We
always loved noodle days at our house.*

*The juice of a lemon sprinkled over buttered noodles is
rather nice. Half a cup of hot cream poured over them isn't
bad either.*

ONION RICE

Norm finds this an easy casserole to serve with a salad and pork
chops, or chicken.

> **2 cups of hot water**
> **1 cup long grain rice**
> **2 tablespoons butter**
> **1 envelope dehydrated onion soup**

Stir all together in a buttered casserole, let stand for 5 minutes,
cover, and cook in a 350°F oven until the rice is tender, about
half an hour or longer.

SOYA RICE

This favourite of Norm's can be used as an accompaniment or could become a main dish by adding shrimp, or chicken, turkey, or ham.

> **1 bunch of green onions, chopped with some of the green tops**
> **1 cup or more celery, diced**
> **2 tablespoons salad oil**
> **2 cups cooked rice**
> **Salt**
> **2 tablespoons or more of soya sauce**
> **Chopped almonds, browned in butter**

Sauté the onions and celery in the oil, but don't brown them. Add the cooked rice, salt, and soya sauce; mix and put in a buttered casserole. Bake at 350°F for 30 minutes, until thoroughly heated. Toss the buttered almonds on top just before serving. I bet you'll make this often.

Mint Jelly

Unless you raise sheep and eat lamb twice a week, buy a bottle of mint jelly when you need it; that's a lot easier than making it.

MINT SAUCE

I've never made it, but my dear and very good editor, Jennifer Glossop, who is also a good cook, has a recipe she uses and will give you.

> **2 tablespoons of mint leaves, finely chopped**
> **½ teaspoon of sugar**
> **3 tablespoons of boiling water**
> **3 tablespoons of malt vinegar**

Combine the mint and sugar in a small bowl. Add the boiling water. Stir and let stand for a few minutes. Add vinegar. Serve at room temperature.

INDEX